Meet Your Chinese Zodiac Animal
中国生肖文化解读系列

The YEAR of the RAT

生肖鼠

Compiled by Zhang Lizhang（张立章）
Translated by Xue Yuwei（薛彧威）& Wu Aijun（吴爱俊）

SinolinguA
华语教学出版社

First Edition 2019

ISBN 978-7-5138-1629-8

Published by Sinolingua Co., Ltd
24 Baiwanzhuang Road, Beijing 100037, China
Tel: (86) 10-68320585 68997826
Fax: (86) 10-68997826 68326333
http://www.sinolingua.com.cn
E-mail: hyjx@sinolingua.com.cn
Facebook: www.facebook.com/sinolingua
Printed by Beijing Xicheng Printing Co., Ltd

Printed in the People's Republic of China

鼠 牛 虎
兔 龍 蛇
馬 羊 猴
鷄 狗 猪

鼠

Introduction

Dear friend, how much do you know about traditional Chinese culture?

Let's try a riddle to start: "There are 12 of them, each person claims but one of them; they can only be found in China. What are they?"

If you can figure it out, it shows that you know something about Chinese culture. In fact, former Japanese Prime Minister Kakuei Tanaka put this riddle to Chinese Premier Zhou Enlai during his visit to China in September 1972 to enliven their meeting. The key to the riddle is "the 12-year cycle of animals in the Chinese zodiac", or simply "the 12 zodiac animals".

The riddle was a piece of cake for Premier Zhou, as the 12 zodiac animals are familiar to everyone in China. But what is the Chinese zodiac?

In Chinese, it is called 生肖 (shēngxiào). 生 means "be born", while 肖 means "resemble". In the eyes of the ancient Chinese, human beings are part of nature. People born in different lunar years correspond to specific animals. A person's character resembles that of his or her animal. The 12 animals are the Rat, Ox, Tiger, Rabbit, Dragon, Snake, Horse, Goat,[①] Monkey, Rooster, Dog and Pig. People thus use them to number the years in a 12-year cycle.

① The Chinese character 羊 (yáng) refers to both the goat and the sheep. Therefore, the eighth zodiac animal can be named goat or sheep. In this book, goat is used for the sake of convenience.

For example, if you were born in 2008, the Year of the Rat, you will have the rat as your zodiac animal and the rat will be your lifelong mascot and guardian angel. Japanese Prime Minister Kakuei Tanaka met Premier Zhou in 1972, which happens to be the Year of the Rat.

The Chinese people often mark the beginning of a year with the Spring Festival, which is the most important festival in the country. It corresponds with one of the 12 zodiac animals, which will in turn become the auspicious image of the festival. Most New Year pictures, couplets, and greetings will feature the zodiac animal.

"In the Year of the Rat, you will have good luck; in the Year of the Ox, you will grow stronger; in the Year of the Tiger, you will behave more bravely; in the Year of the Rabbit, you will become smarter; in the Year of the Dragon, you will have a promising career; in the Year of the Snake, you will be safe and sound; in the Year of the Horse, you will live a brilliant life; in the Year of the Goat, you will enjoy prosperity; in the Year of the Monkey, you will get a promotion; in the Year of the Rooster, you will win a prize; in the Year of the Dog, you will flourish; in the Year of the Pig, you will become more prominent." This is a Chinese

New Year greeting related to the 12 zodiac animals used to wish everyone the best every year.

In China, there is a tradition associated with the Spring Festival that has been handed down for over a thousand years. When meeting with people during the festival, one should offer felicitations to others as often as possible. If instead you were to utter something ominous, it is said that this utterance will come true. In addition, Chinese people often use different felicitations in different years. If the year happens to be a year of a zodiac animal that has a noble status based on Chinese traditional culture, a good image, or a name that shares a similar pronunciation with words portending good fortune, Chinese people will use the zodiac animal name in their New Year greetings. These zodiac animals are the Ox, Tiger,

Rabbit, Dragon, Horse, Goat, Monkey, and Rooster. As for the other zodiac animals, which are the Rat, Snake, Dog and Pig, they do not appear in New Year greetings. So when the Spring Festival for the Year of the Rat comes, how do Chinese people offer their greetings? Actually, they replace 鼠年 (the Year of the Rat) with 新年 (New Year) or 新春 (New Year Spring Festival) in their greetings.

1. Happy New Year!

（祝您）新年快乐！(Zhù nín) Xīnnián kuàilè!

2. I wish you every luck in the New Year!

祝您新年大吉！Zhù nín Xīnnián dà jí!

3. I wish you great fortune in the New Year!

祝您新年发大财，行大运！

Zhù nín Xīnnián fā dà cái, xíng dà yùn!

4. I wish you all the best in the New Year!

祝您新年万事如意！Zhù nín Xīnnián wànshì-rúyì!

引 言

亲爱的朋友，您对中国传统文化是否了解？

请您先猜个谜语。谜面是：共有12个，每人占一个，东洋西洋都没有，请问是什么？

如果你猜出了正确答案，说明你对中国文化有一定的了解。这个谜语是1972年9月日本前首相田中角荣先生访华时，为活跃气氛给时任中国总理的周恩来先生猜的一个谜语。谜底就是："12生肖"。

这个谜语没能难住周恩来总理，因为每个中国人都熟知12生肖。那么，什么是中国人的"生肖"呢？

"生肖"的"生"就是"出生"的意思，"肖"是"相似"的意思。也就是说，在中国古人的观念里，作为自然界的普通一员，不同时间出生的人，就会与某一种动物相对应，其性格也会与该动物的特征相似。这些动物分别是鼠、牛、虎、兔、龙、蛇、马、羊、猴、鸡、狗、猪，共12种。中国人就用这12种动物来纪年，12年一个循环，周而复始。

如果你出生在2008年，那一年正是鼠年，那么你的属相就是鼠，鼠便成为你一生的吉祥物和保护神。开篇故事中的两位主角会面的1972年恰巧是中国的鼠年。

中国人以自己的传统节日——春节为一年之始，而每一年的春节都以当年对应的生肖动物作为节日图腾。春节张贴的年画、春联和新年祝福语都会以此为主题。

“鼠年运来，牛年身壮，虎年勇猛，兔年机巧，龙年飞腾，蛇年安康，马年奔放，羊年开泰，猴年高升，鸡年中奖，狗年兴旺，猪年响当当！”这就是一句以12生肖为主题的新年祝福语，寓意是“年年你都会有好运气”。

中国人有一个流传千百年的文化传统，就是在春节前后，见人要多说吉利话。传说如果在这个佳节期间说不吉利的话会应验成真。但是，不同生肖年的春节，中国人常用的吉利话也有所不同：在中国文化传统中地位高、形象好，或者谐音吉利的生肖动物就会直接出现在吉祥话中，比如牛、虎、兔、龙、马、羊、猴、鸡；另外一些生肖动物并不适宜出现在吉利话中，如鼠、蛇、狗、猪等。那么，在鼠年春节，中国人会怎么说这些吉利话呢？一般会用“新年、新春”代替“鼠年”。

1. （祝您）新年快乐！
2. 祝您新年大吉！
3. 祝您新年发大财，行大运！
4. 祝您新年万事如意！

Contents
目录

Chapter Three

Chapter Four

子
丑
寅
卯
辰
巳
午
未
申
酉
戌
亥

Chapter One

Zodiac Culture in Everyday Chinese Life

The long-cherished Chinese zodiac tradition has been passed down from generation to generation and has become deep-rooted in people's minds. It is widely recognized among the Chinese people that the 12 zodiac animal signs are closely linked with people's personalities, destinies, lives and careers. Just as British people might talk about the weather when they first meet, Chinese people often ask what zodiac animal a person is when they meet for the first time. This can be explained for the following reasons:

First, it is a good way to deduce the age of a person. Since it's not very polite to ask another person's age directly, their zodiac animal coupled with their appearance can help one deduce a person's age.

Second, it serves as an ice-breaker and makes people feel at ease. Asking about zodiac animals is considered a common communication skill by Chinese people. When two people find they share the same zodiac animal, they will have a natural

affinity and be eager to talk with each other.

Chinese people tend to group themselves according to their zodiac animal signs out of the belief that those with the same sign possess similar personalities and characteristics. Hence, they like discussing in which zodiac animal year a prominent figure was born in their spare time. They even consider it a great honor if they find that they happen to share the same zodiac sign with a renowned historical figure or contemporary celebrity, such as Genghis Khan (born in the Year of the Horse), founder of the Mongol Empire; Zhuge Liang (born in the Year of the Rooster), a statesman during the period of the Three Kingdoms (220-280) and a paradigm of wisdom and good virtue; Li Shimin (born in the Year of the Goat), the co-founder of the Tang Dynasty (618-907), a golden age in Chinese history; Deng Xiaoping (born in the Year of the Dragon), the late Chinese leader regarded as the chief architect of China's reform and opening-up; and Xi Jinping (born in the Year of the Snake), the current Chinese President.

Third, it can help people extrapolate other people's personalities. According to zodiac animal culture, people born in the same zodiac animal year often share similar personality traits, luck for wealth, professional achievements and marriage patterns. Some Chinese people even get to know and choose their spouses, co-workers or business partners by talking about their zodiac animals. This topic seems simple, but it has rich connotations to the Chinese people.

If you are born in the Year of the Rat, what kind of character, luck and marriage will you have according to the Chinese zodiac? Please read the following introduction and see if it is true for you.

十二生肖

Characteristics of "Rats"

In China, it is believed that people born in the Year of the Rat are diligent and are prudent in dealing with financial matters; blessed with good fortune, they seldom have to worry about money; they often have successful careers.

People born in the Year of the Rat are known for their agility, energy and vitality. They are able to easily adapt to the changing circumstances. Being kind-hearted, quick-witted and sensible, they are also resourceful, considerate and versatile. They often enjoy great popularity among people thanks to their lively and optimistic character.

However, people born in the Year of the Rat often lack courage and resolve. They are not good at innovation or pioneering jobs. They are adept at speculating, known for being hypercritical and are also narrow-minded.

Marriages for "Rats"

Chinese people often believe that if the zodiac animals of a couple are a good match, they will enjoy a loving relationship and a happy life; if they are not a good match,

十二生肖

a marriage may not be satisfactory. For instance, if a person is born in the Years of the Rat, the best match for him or her is a person born in the years of the ox, dragon, monkey and pig. However, if he or she marries a person born in the Year of the Goat, they may be prone to bickering.

You may have never realized that this notion has exerted great influence on people's attitudes towards marriage for nearly two thousand years. During the Qing Dynasty (1616-1911) and dynasties before that, marriages were arranged by parents, while people themselves had no freedom to choose their spouses. People often considered the match of zodiac animals as one of the important factors in determining a marriage. This resulted in a great number of tragic marriages during the long period of feudalism in China. However, young people today no longer cling to the match of zodiac animals when they choose

their boyfriends or girlfriends. At any rate, this remains an indispensable topic for chitchat among Chinese people.

Eminent Figures Born in the Year of the Rat

According to the Chinese zodiac, many outstanding historical figures were born in the Year of the Rat, for example:

Zhuangzi

Born in 369 BC, a philosopher and thinker during the Warring States Period (475-221 BC).

Du Fu

Born in 712, known as the poet-sage of the Tang Dynasty.

Li Qingzhao

Born in 1084, a famous poetess of the Song Dynasty (960-1279).

Zhu Di

Born in 1360, an emperor who seized power and established Beijing as the capital during the Ming Dynasty (1368-1644).

Kong Shangren

Born in 1648, the 64th-generation descendant of Confucius and a Ming Dynasty dramatist best known for his play *The Peach Blossom Fan.*

Qigong

Born in 1912, a contemporary calligrapher, painter and connoisseur of cultural relics.

In other countries, there are also many distinguished figures who were born in the Year of the Rat. Some of them are listed below. Look into whether or not they also share the hallmark characteristics of the "Rat".

Ferdinand Magellan

Born in 1480, the famous Portuguese navigator who was the first explorer in history to accomplish a circumnavigation of the globe.

William Shakespeare

Born in 1564, the greatest English playwright and poet.

Galileo Galilei

Born in 1564, the renowned Italian astronomer who is hailed as the "father of modern science".

Peter the Great

Born in 1672, the first emperor of the Russian Empire.

George Washington

Born in 1732, the first President of the United States.

Wolfgang Amadeus Mozart

Born in 1756, an Austrian musician.

Ludwig Feuerbach

Born in 1804, the renowned German philosopher.

Leo Tolstoy

Born in 1828, one of the most celebrated Russian writers of the 19th century.

Pyotr Ilyich Tchaikovsky

Born in 1840, a Russian composer.

Auguste Rodin

Born in 1840, a renowned French sculptor.

Claude Monet

Born in 1840, one of the founders of the French Impressionist school.

Mutsuhito

Born in 1852, the Emperor of Japan, known as Emperor Meiji, who launched the Meiji Restoration there in 1868.

第一章 中国人生活中的生肖文化

生肖文化在中国历史悠久，世代相传，家喻户晓，早已深深根植于中国人的血液之中。它与每个中国人的性格、命运、生活和事业紧密联系在一起，并得到中国人的普遍认同。直到今天，人们初次见面时，问询对方的生肖也是常事，如同英国人见面谈论天气一样普通。这主要有以下几方面的原因：

一是通过询问生肖来推测对方的实际年龄。因为直接询问对方的年龄不太礼貌，所以可以通过间接询问对方的生肖后，再根据外貌特征显示的年龄范围基本可以确定对方的实际年龄。

二是谈论生肖可迅速打破尴尬，拉近双方的心理距离。这也是中国人常见的一种见面沟通技巧，尤其是当生肖相同时，两人就有了天然的亲近感，话题自然打开。

在工作、生活中，中国人会不自觉地按照同一个生肖划分出了小群体，以显得亲近。闲暇时人们还喜欢聊聊中国某一著名人物的生肖，还会以与历史伟人或当代名人的生肖相同而沾沾自喜。比如：蒙古帝国的缔造者——成吉思汗属马；被中国人公认为智慧与品德典范的三国时期政治家——诸葛亮属鸡；中国古代最繁荣的王朝“大唐盛世”的开创者——李世民属羊；被誉为当代“中国社会主义现代化建设和改革开放总设计师”的前国家领导人——邓小平属龙；现任中国国家领导人——习近平属蛇；等等。

三是根据生肖来推测对方的性格类型及特点。中国人认为，相同生肖的人往往具有类似的性格、财运、事业成就和婚姻状况等。一些中国人就是在谈论生肖的过程中了解、选择自己的婚恋对象、同事搭档和创业伙伴的。这个看似简单的生肖话题，却被中国人赋予了如此丰富多样的内涵。

按照中国生肖文化的观念，属鼠人有着特定的性格、运气和婚姻状况。假如你是属鼠的，你可以对照一下自己，看有哪些特点与你相契合。

一、属鼠人的性格特点

中国人认为，属鼠人一般较为勤劳，能够谨慎处理金钱，财运也好，一生中很少会遇到金钱上的困扰，事业上颇有成就。

在性格方面，属鼠人感觉敏锐、反应快捷、精力充沛、活力十足，有很强的环境适应力和应变能力；属鼠人本性善良，机智、主意多、识时务，多才多艺且善解人意，爽朗活泼、讨人喜爱，多数属于乐天派性格。

此外，属鼠人存在做事缺少胆识、魄力不够的缺点，创新性和开拓性不足，易投机取巧，爱挑剔，心胸不够宽大。

二、属鼠人的姻缘

在恋爱、婚姻观念方面，中国生肖匹配观念十分奇特：如果生肖匹配，夫妻二人就会感情深厚、婚姻幸福；否则，就不如人意。属鼠的人，最适宜寻求生肖为牛、龙、猴和猪的人作为结婚对象；如果与属羊的人搭配就容易发生争吵。

或许你没有想到，这种传统的婚姻选择观念已经影响了中国人近两千年。在以前的封建王朝时代，婚姻双方当事人没有自由选择的权利，父母是儿女婚姻的绝对决定者，而男女双方的生肖是否匹配是能否结婚的重要依据之一。没有人知道，在中国漫长的封建时代里，非自由选择的婚姻模式到底酿成了多少婚姻悲剧！当然，这些早已成为了历史，今天的年轻人已不再执着于生肖相配的恋爱观，可这些仍旧是中国人茶余饭后交流沟通中必不可少的内容。

三、属鼠的中外名人

按照中国人的生肖算法，中国历史上鼠年出生的杰出人物非常多。例如：

战国时代哲学家、思想家——庄子（公元前369年出生）；

被誉为“诗圣”的唐代诗人——杜甫（712年出生）；

宋代著名女词人——李清照（1084年出生）；

明代以武力夺取皇位、建都北京的明成祖——朱棣（1360出生）；

明代戏曲作家、孔子第64代孙、戏曲名作《桃花扇》作者——孔尚任（1648年出生）；

当代书法家、画家、文物鉴定家——启功（1912年出生）；

中国以外，鼠年出生的各国杰出人物也不少。下面列举一些世界名人，你可以研究一下他们是否有生肖鼠的性格特点。

第一次实现环球航行的葡萄牙航海家——麦哲伦（1480 年出生）；

英国最伟大的戏剧家——莎士比亚（1564 年出生）；

被誉为“近代科学之父”的意大利天文学家——伽利略（1564 年出生）；

沙俄首位皇帝——彼得大帝（1672 年出生）；

美国第一任总统——华盛顿（1732 年出生）；

奥地利著名音乐家——莫扎特(1756 年出生)；

德国唯物主义哲学家——费尔巴哈（1804 年出生）；

俄国 19 世纪伟大的作家——托尔斯泰（1828 年出生）；

俄国著名作曲家——柴可夫斯基（1840 年出生）；

法国著名雕塑家——罗丹（1840 年出生）；

法国印象画派创始人之一——莫奈（1840年出生）；

实施“明治维新”的日本明治天皇——睦仁（1852年出生）。

Chapter Two

The Origin and Cultural Significance of the Chinese Zodiac Animals

Methods of Year Designation in Ancient China

The Chinese people invented their calendar very early on. During the Xia Dynasty (c.2070-1600 BC), a fairly precise calendar was created. This is why the traditional Chinese calendar was also called the Xia calendar. This Xia calendar, however, was used to designate months rather than years and served as a guide for agricultural production and sacrificial activities. In China, the practice of designating years began during the Western Zhou Dynasty (1046-771 BC). Three methods of year designation were later developed, designating years by emperors' reign titles, by Heavenly Stems and Earthly Branches, and by Chinese zodiac animals respectively.

Emperor Wudi of Han (140-88 BC)

I. Using the emperor's reign title to designate a year

This method of designating years dates back to the reign of Emperor Wudi (140-88 BC) of the Western Han Dynasty. From then on, an emperor could adopt several reign titles. For example, Emperor Wudi of Han adopted eleven titles. During the Ming and Qing dynasties, an emperor could only adopt one reign title. A new emperor had to designate a different title in the following year after he ascended to the throne and keep that title until he abdicated or died. This convention continued until 1912, when the last emperor of the Qing Dynasty, Puyi, abdicated (Puyi's reign title was Xuantong). The practice of using the emperor's reign title to designate a year ended with the abolition of China's feudal monarchy.

II. Using Heavenly Stems and Earthly Branches to designate a year

Ancient Chinese chose ten astronomical phenomena and gave them a collective name of Heavenly Stems, which are referred to as 甲 (jiǎ) , 乙 (yǐ) , 丙 (bǐng) , 丁 (dīng) , 戊 (wù) , 己 (jǐ) , 庚 (gēng) , 辛 (xīn) , 壬 (rén) and 癸 (guǐ) . They have also been used as serial numbers. People in ancient China also divided the orbit of Jupiter revolving around the sun into 12 parts and gave them a collective name Earthly Branches, which includes 子 (zǐ), 丑 (chǒu), 寅 (yín), 卯 (mǎo), 辰 (chén), 巳 (sì), 午 (wǔ), 未 (wèi), 申 (shēn), 酉 (yǒu), 戌 (xū) and 亥 (hài). The ten Heavenly Stems and 12 Earthly Branches form 60 pairs in total, thus this year designation method adopts 60 years as a cycle with

甲子 (jiǎzǐ) as the first and 癸亥 (guǐhài) the last.

III. Using the Chinese zodiac to designate a year

The Chinese adopted the zodiac year designation during the Han Dynasty (206 BC-AD 220) with 12 years as a cycle. It was a novel approach to use the 12 animals to mark each year, making it easier for people to remember every year. After this approach was adopted, everyone had their own zodiac animal based on the year in which they were born. This is the beginning of the rich and unique zodiac culture created by the Chinese people.

The Gregorian calendar has been adopted in China to officially designate the year since the founding of the People's Republic of China in 1949. But the method of using the Chinese zodiac for year designation is still popular among the Chinese people. For example, 2008 is called a rat year, and the next rat year will be 2020.

Origin of the Chinese Zodiac Animals

Why did the Chinese ancestors choose the Rat, Ox, Tiger, Rabbit, Dragon, Snake, Horse, Goat, Monkey, Rooster, Dog and Pig to be on their zodiac? How did their sequence come about? There is a popular legend among the Chinese people that explains it.

Once upon a time, the immortal Great White Golden Star reported to the Jade Emperor (the supreme God in Chinese mythology who ruled all the immortals and spirits in heaven and on earth) that people on earth didn't have a method to calculate the year and month, thus he proposed a convenient year designation method be devised to make it easier for people to plant and harvest crops based on seasonal changes. His advice was welcomed by the emperor, who then appointed an official to be in charge of zodiac affairs and to organize a river-crossing contest for animals. The rules were that the 12 animals that crossed the river and reached the Heavenly Palace first would be granted titles as the 12 Chinese zodiac animals. Their sequence was to be decided by their places in the contest.

News of the contest spread far and wide. The animals who came for registration formed a long queue.

The contest produced many interesting stories.

Story One

The Cat and the Rat Become Enemies

Once upon a time, the cat and the rat were close friends. The cat always stayed in bed every morning until the rat woke him up. On the eve of the contest, the cat urged the rat time and again to wake him up the next morning. The rat readily agreed. The next morning, the rat got up very early and saw the cat still sound asleep. Instead of waking him up, the rat snuck away and hit the road on his own. The cat eventually woke up late and missed the contest. From then on, the cat harbored hatred towards the rat. The cat would chase rats at any sight of one.

Story Two

The Simple-minded Ox

As the rat was rushing to the contest, he encountered the old ox. The clever rat quickly ran to the ox and begged him to help him cross the river. He promised that he wouldn't compete against the ox for first place. The kind, but simple-minded ox agreed and asked the rat to sit on his head. The contest began and he used all of his strength to swim to the other side of the river. As they were approaching the bank, the rat exerted himself and jumped on shore. He then ran towards the finish line before the ox had even reached the riverbank. The rat was the winner while the ox came second in the contest.

Story Three

The Dragon Fails to Become Champion

The dragon had dominion over all the waters and was quite adept at swimming, so how did he fail to become champion? It turned out that right before his departure, he found the land to the west of a mountain was suffering from a drought and the crops people planted were withering. Therefore, the conscientious dragon set off for the Eastern Sea to first fetch water and provide some timely rain for the area west of the mountain. Consequently, he was late for the contest and came in fifth place.

Story Four

The Smart Little Rabbit

Since the rabbit was not a good swimmer, he needed to find another way to cross the river. The quick-witted rabbit hit upon a great idea just one day before the contest: He took a long rope and tied one end of it to a tree on the bank; then he asked the turtle to tie the other end to another tree across the river. When the contest started, the rabbit grabbed the rope and crawled to the other side of the river. He crossed the river without even getting his fur wet.

Story Five

The Goat, the Monkey and the Rooster Help Each Other

The goat, the monkey and the rooster formed a team to help each other cross the river. They found some bamboo poles and ropes and used them to make a raft; then they made two wooden oars out of a plank. When the contest kicked off, the rooster stood in the front to guide the direction while the monkey and the goat sat side by side and paddled hard with the oars. Thanks to their concerted efforts, the three crossed the wide river very quickly.

Story Six

The Last Winner

Many contestants had crossed the river and arrived at the Heavenly Palace. The zodiac official counted but found there were only 11 animals present. Everyone thus kept a close eye on who would turn up as the last winner. Suddenly, a snort was heard — a little pig was coming. The official looked at the pig who was gasping for breath and asked, "Why are you so late?" The pig blushed with shame and replied, "I'm fond of eating and sleeping, which made me grow so fat that I'm no match for them in swimming." Hearing what the pig said, everybody burst into laughter.

申

Perfect Ending

The Jade Emperor announced the contest result: the 12 zodiac animals were sequenced as Rat, Ox, Tiger, Rabbit, Dragon, Snake, Horse, Goat, Monkey, Rooster, Dog and Pig. Since then, the Chinese people have adopted the 12 zodiac animals to designate the years which helped them lead a more regular life and engage in farming appropriately according to seasonal changes.

Now let's return from folklore to reality. In fact, an important reason why the ancient Chinese selected these 12 animals from the thousands available was perhaps that they had discovered the shining points in each of them.

Some experts believe that recording time is a major factor contributing to the appearance of the 12 zodiac animals. The ancient astronomers used to divide one day into 12 double hours, namely 子时 (zǐshí), 丑时 (chǒushí), 寅时 (yínshí), 卯时 (mǎoshí), 辰时 (chénshí), 巳时 (sìshí), 午时 (wǔshí), 未时 (wèishí), 申时 (shēnshí), 酉时 (yǒushí), 戌时 (xūshí), 亥时 (hàishí), according to the order of the Earthly Branches. Ancient Chinese selected 12 animals as the zodiac signs and determined their order based on the animals' living habits and routine activities at different times each day.

子时 is from 11:00 pm to 1:00 am the next day. It is in the dead of night, and rats move around rampantly at this time. Hence the Rat (鼠 , shǔ) stands for 子时, and is called 子鼠 (zǐshǔ).

丑时 is from 1:00 am to 3:00 am. Farmers often wake up at this time and feed oxen grass by lamplight. Due to this, the Ox (牛 , niú) corresponds with 丑时, and is called 丑牛 (chǒuniú).

寅时 is from 3:00 am to 5:00 am. The nocturnal tigers are quite ferocious, and ancient Chinese could often hear their howls at this time. Because of this, the Tiger (虎 , hǔ) represents 寅时, and is called 寅虎 (yínhǔ).

卯时 is from 5:00 am to 7:00 am. As the day breaks at this time, rabbits often go out of their burrows to eat the green grass covered with morning dew. Therefore, the Rabbit (兔 , tù) stands for 卯时, and is called 卯兔 (mǎotù).

辰时 is from 7:00 am to 9:00 am. The sun rises, and it often gets foggy at this time. Legend has it that the dragon is fond of riding on clouds and mists which go farther up the sky when the sun rises, representing an upward and promising life. Therefore, the Dragon (龙 , lóng) represents 辰时, and is called 辰龙 (chénlóng).

巳时 is from 9:00 am to 11:00 am. When the fog lifts and the sun rises at this time, the snake often crawls out of its cave to look for food. Therefore, the Snake (蛇 , shé) is also called 巳蛇 (sìshé).

午时 is from 11:00 am to 1:00 pm. The ancient wild horse enjoyed neighing and galloping around at noon before it was tamed by human beings. Therefore, the Horse (马 , mǎ) is called 午马 (wǔmǎ).

未时 is from 1:00 pm to 3:00 pm. Shepherds believe it is best to graze goats at this time, so ancient Chinese associated this period with the goats and offered the zodiac animal Goat (羊 , yáng) another name: 未羊 (wèiyáng).

申时 is from 3:00 pm to 5:00 pm. This is the time just before sunset when the day becomes cooler, which is why the monkey likes climbing trees and yelping in them at this time. Therefore, 申时 corresponds with the Monkey (猴 , hóu), which is also called 申猴 (shēnhóu).

酉时 is from 5:00 pm to 7:00 pm. As the sun sets at this time, the rooster often wanders around in front of its nest. Therefore, the Rooster (鸡 , jī) is also called 酉鸡 (yǒujī).

戌时 is from 7:00 pm to 9:00 pm. This is the time when people lock their doors after a busy day's work, getting ready to rest, and when a dog often stays in front of a house and guards it. If something unusual occurs, it will bark to alert its master. Therefore, the Dog (狗 , gǒu) can also be called 戌狗 (xūgǒu).

亥时 is from 9:00 pm to 11:00 pm. In the still of night, the sleeping sound of pigs can be heard. Therefore, 亥时 is represented by the Pig (猪 , zhū) , which is also called 亥猪 (hàizhū).

By matching the 12 double hours with their corresponding animals, the 12 zodiac animals came into being: Rat, Ox, Tiger, Rabbit, Dragon, Snake, Horse, Goat, Monkey, Rooster, Dog and Pig. Thereafter, ancient Chinese adopted the 12 zodiac animals to record time and years. Since then, a rich culture associated with the 12 zodiac animals has gradually evolved.

Zodiac Animals and the Corresponding 12 Earthly Branches

No.	Earthly Branch	Zodiac Animal
1	*zi* 子	Rat 鼠
2	*chou* 丑	Ox 牛
3	*yin* 寅	Tiger 虎
4	*mao* 卯	Rabbit 兔
5	*chen* 辰	Dragon 龙
6	*si* 巳	Snake 蛇
7	*wu* 午	Horse 马
8	*wei* 未	Goat 羊
9	*shen* 申	Monkey 猴
10	*you* 酉	Rooster 鸡
11	*xu* 戌	Dog 狗
12	*hai* 亥	Pig 猪

The Wisdom Behind the Chinese Zodiac Culture

Confucianism can be viewed as the mainstream of traditional Chinese culture, and the "Doctrine of the Mean" is deemed the essence of Confucianism. By following the "Doctrine of the Mean", or the "Middle Course", the Chinese people strive to be impartial and behave with a sense of propriety. The Chinese

idiom过犹不及 (guòyóubùjí), meaning "too much is as bad as too little", can be seen as a good interpretation of the "Doctrine of the Mean". Every coin has two sides. If overdone, a person's strength may take a turn and become his shortcoming. Therefore, by matching the Chinese zodiac animals in pairs, our ancestors were actually hoping to make people aware of their own traits while gaining something from others' strengths in the process of improving themselves. Nowadays, Chinese people hope to work with or marry someone whose personalities are different from their own, so as to achieve a balance. In addition, the match of the zodiac animals as shown in the following pages serves as an example to explain the subtle relationship between craftiness and industriousness, bravery and wisdom, low and high profiles, ambition and modesty, resilience and perseverance, and amity and loyalty in traditional Chinese culture.

No. One

Rat and Ox

The rat is known for its quick wit and vigilance; the ox is characterized by its honesty and diligence. As a popular Chinese saying goes, "What a cow eats is nothing but grass, but what it produces is milk." Traditional Chinese values praise the rat's resourcefulness while at the same time upholding the ox's spirit of dedication. If a man relies too much on his cunning, he may tend to be an opportunist and not perform actual deeds; if someone buries himself in hard work, yet lacks the use of skill and method, he may labor hard, but to little avail. Therefore, a wise person should be able to combine his resourcefulness and diligence.

No. Two

Tiger and Rabbit

In Chinese folklore, the tiger has long been regarded as the king of all animals and the epitome of bravery and courage; the little rabbit is a representative of small and weak animals and is known for its prudence and intellect. If a person always takes reckless actions, his bravery will turn into rudeness and invite trouble sooner or later; however, someone who is overcautious may lack the courage to surmount difficulties, making him a coward who is unable to achieve anything. Therefore, the Chinese people consider bravery and prudence two complementary merits a person should possess.

No. Three

Dragon and Snake

The dragon, the mythical animal created by the ancient Chinese people, has been endowed with supreme power and status. It is often used as a metaphor of someone who is in his palmy days and enjoys the best of his time. The snake has been called the "little dragon" because it was demoted to the earth from heaven for breaking the law. Having lost the status of dragon and omnipotent strength, the snake became a synonym for stoicism and kept a low profile. The transformation between the dragon and the snake can be viewed as a real picture of one's life with both high and low points. The character of these two animals may lead to two extremes, and as such, the match of them is a manifestation of the "Doctrine of the Mean" upheld by the Chinese: avoid arrogance in success; don't lose heart in frustration.

No. Four

Horse and Goat

Since ancient times, the horse has been deemed the epitome of enterprising spirit and accomplishment. Those with such merits are often likened by the Chinese people to a "fine steed", which means they are someone with remarkable talent. The goat is praised for its modesty and kindness. In Chinese, idioms containing the character 马 (mǎ, horse) take up the most proportion of phrases related to the zodiac animals, and the majority of them have the meaning of "marching ahead courageously". The goat usually appears in folk stories featuring the theme of kindness and modesty. Therefore, the Chinese often wish to acquire the qualities of both animals.

No.Five

Monkey and Rooster

Characterized by their intelligence and flexibility, some monkeys may be as smart as toddlers in certain aspects. The rooster crows at dawn all year round in all weather. With no clock to use in ancient times, Chinese farmers often relied on the rooster's crow as their wake-up call. Therefore, in the eyes of the Chinese people, the monkey is the epitome of intelligence and flexibility, while the rooster is seen as a perfect example of perseverance. They uphold the view of "acting according to the changing circumstances" while being aware that only through persistent efforts can one achieve success. Given this, we should try to strike a balance between the monkey's flexibility and the rooster's perseverance.

No.Six

Dog and Pig

As man's best friend, a dog will never leave its master even when faced with hunger and death. Pigs, on the contrary, do not care about choosing a master, but rather indulge in eating and sleeping. As a result, pigs are used to refer to people who go with the flow and those who lead a carefree life. Among the Chinese zodiac animals, the dog is the epitome of loyalty and faithfulness while the pig stands for fortune and luck. The Chinese value the dog's loyalty as well as its merit of not despising the poor and currying favor with the rich; meanwhile, they also have an admiration for the pig as it seems to be endowed with good luck.

Can we say the values of the Chinese people are paradoxical? In fact, such seemingly contradictory values are an essential part of Chinese culture. The aforementioned zodiac pairs fully embody the "art of balance" and the pursuit of perfection in Chinese culture.

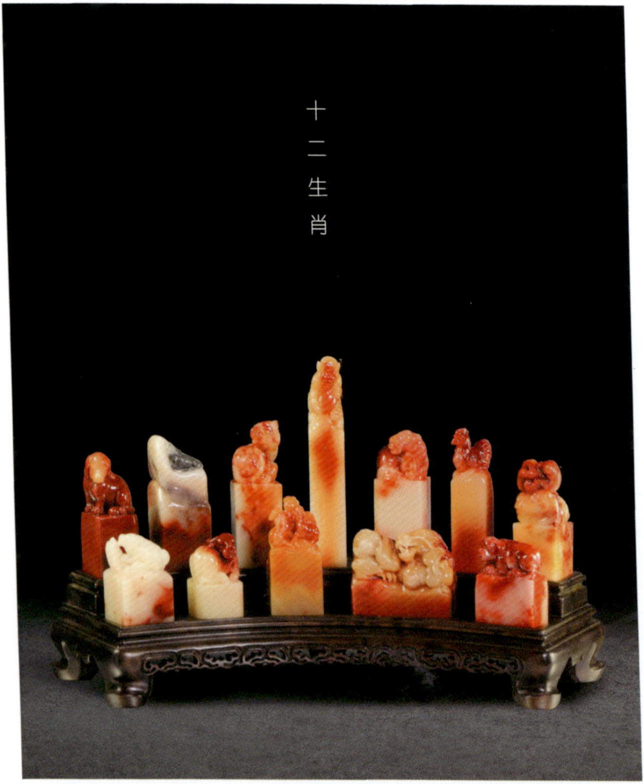

第二章 中国12生肖文化起源与内涵

一、中国古代纪年法

中国人很早就创造了历法。大约在中国的夏朝（约公元前2070—公元前1600）时就拥有较为准确的历法，因此，中国传统历法被称为夏历。但夏历并不是用来纪年，而是用来纪月、指导安排农业生产和各种祭祀活动的。中国最早的纪年大约是从西周（公元前1046—公元前771）时期开始的，渐渐形成三种主要的纪年方法：帝王年号纪年法、干支纪年法和生肖纪年法。

第一种纪年法是采用皇帝年号纪年。中国采用帝王年号纪年法始于西汉汉武帝（公元前140—公元前88）。从汉武帝开始，一位皇帝可以使用多个年号，汉武帝在位时期就用过11个年号。到了明清时期，才逐渐演变为一位皇帝一个年号。新皇帝登基第二年启用新年号纪年，直至皇帝退位或去世。这种纪年法一直持续到1912年中国清王朝最后一个皇帝——溥仪退位（纪年年号为“宣统”），才随着中国封建帝制的结束而永远成为了历史。

第二种纪年法是使用干支纪年。中国古人选取

10种天象作为列举事物的次序号，称为“天干”。其名称分别是“甲、乙、丙、丁、戊、己、庚、辛、壬、癸”。中国古人又把木星围绕太阳公转的轨道划分为12个部分，称为“地支”。其名称分别是“子、丑、寅、卯、辰、巳、午、未、申、酉、戌、亥”。10个天干与12个地支排列组合数为60，于是干支纪年法就以60年为一个循环周期。纪年从甲子开始，以癸亥结束，周而复始。

第三种纪年法是用12个生肖动物纪年。中国民间大约从汉朝（公元前206—公元220）就开始使用12生肖来纪年，12年一循环。以12种生肖动物来纪年简单易记、形象生动。每人因出生年而自然对应一种动物，由此中国人创造出内容丰富、独具特色的生肖文化。

1949年中华人民共和国成立后，中国官方开始采用国际上通用的公元纪年法。中国民间则依然盛行生肖纪年方法，自古沿用至今。比如2008年为鼠年，下一个鼠年将是2020年。

二、中国12生肖的来历传说

中国人的祖先为什么挑选鼠、牛、虎、兔、龙、蛇、马、羊、猴、鸡、狗、猪这12种动物作为生肖动物呢？顺序又是如何排定的呢？在中国民间，流传着一个家喻户晓的传说故事。

一天，天神太白金星向玉皇大帝（中国神话中天庭和人间所有鬼神的总首领）报告，人间的老百姓没有计算年月的方法。他建议制定一个简单易行的纪年方法，以方便天下百姓按照时节耕种、收获庄稼。玉皇大帝认为这个建议非常好。于是他任命一名生肖官，负责组织一场动物过河比赛，最先过河到达天宫的12种动物会被册封为12生肖，生肖的排位顺序按照比赛名次确定。

渡河比赛获胜可以成为12生肖的消息很快传开，前来报名的动物们排起了长长的队伍。

在比赛过程中发生了许多有趣的小故事。

故事1：猫与老鼠结仇

猫和老鼠本来是一对形影不离的好朋友。平时，猫总爱睡懒觉，早上都是老鼠叫它起床。比赛前一天晚上，猫再三叮嘱老鼠明早记着叫醒它，老鼠满口答应了。第二天早晨，老鼠早早地就起了床，看了看还在熟睡的猫，却没有叫醒它，自己悄悄地上路了。猫醒来后没有赶上生肖比赛，从此就恨上了老鼠，见老鼠就抓。

故事 2：憨厚老牛上当

老鼠在急匆匆去参加比赛的路上碰到了老牛。机灵的老鼠急忙跑到老牛身边，可怜兮兮地请求老牛帮助它渡河，还信誓旦旦地保证决不跟老牛抢第一名！善良憨厚的老牛答应了老鼠的请求，让老鼠坐到它的头上。比赛开始了，老牛使出全身力气向河对岸游去。在临近河岸时，没等老牛上岸，老鼠“嗖”的一声第一个跳上了岸，一溜烟似的跑了。老鼠成了第一名，老牛只好屈居第二。

故事 3：龙痛失冠军

掌管水务、最擅长游泳的龙为什么没能取得第一名呢？原来龙在临出发前，发现大山以西土地干旱，老百姓的庄稼都快干死了。于是，负责任的龙先到东海取水，再到大山之西去降雨，等赶回来参加比赛时已经迟到了，所以龙只取得第五名的成绩。

故事4：小兔巧妙过河

那么，小兔子不擅长游泳，该怎么过河呢？爱动脑筋的小兔子终于在比赛的前一天想出了一个好方法：它找来一条长长的绳子，先把绳子拴在河边的一棵树上，再请河龟帮忙把绳子的另一头拴在河对岸的另一棵树上。第二天比赛时，小兔子紧紧抓住这条绳子，顺着绳子爬过了河，没有沾到一滴水。

故事5：山羊、猴子和公鸡团队合作

山羊、猴子和公鸡结成团队，共同想办法过河。它们找来一些竹竿和细绳，做成竹筏，用木板做成两支划水的木桨。比赛时，公鸡站在竹筏前头引导方向，猴子和山羊坐在竹筏的左右两边，用木桨使劲划水。它们齐心协力，很快就渡过了宽宽的大河。

故事6：最后一名幸运者

参赛的动物们先后渡过了河，到达了天宫。生肖官仔细一数，只有11种动物。于是，大家都伸长了脖子，想看看到底是谁将幸运地得到这最后一个名额。突然，大家听见“哼、哼”的声音，原来是小猪来了。生肖官看着气喘吁吁的小猪，问道："你为什么来得这么晚啊？"小猪不好意思地回答说："我平时贪吃，又爱睡觉，身体有点胖，所以游泳比不过它们。"大家都哈哈大笑了起来。

完美结局

玉皇大帝郑重地宣布比赛结果：12 生肖排名依次是鼠、牛、虎、兔、龙、蛇、马、羊、猴、鸡、狗、猪。从此，人间的百姓就有了用 12 生肖纪年的方法，生活起居有规律，播种和收获庄稼、菜蔬、花木等皆有时节。

现在，我们从 12 生肖动物渡河比赛的神话故事中回归现实。中国古人从千百种常见动物中选定这 12 种动物的重要原因，或许是看中这 12 种动物身上各具不同的优点。

一些专家认为，12 生肖产生的原因主要是出于记时的需要。古代天文学家将一昼夜分为 12 个时辰，每个时辰为两个小时，并按照地支的顺序分别命名为"子时、丑时、寅时、卯时、辰时、巳时、午时、未时、申时、酉时、戌时、亥时"。中国古人就依照生活中观察到不同时间段内动物的行为习惯和活动规律，确定了12生肖顺序。

夜间11点至次日凌晨1点，属子时，正是老鼠趁夜深人静频繁活动之时。因此，子时对应生肖动物为鼠，故称“子鼠”。

凌晨1点至3点，属丑时。牛习惯夜间吃草，农民就会在深夜起床来挑灯喂牛。因此，丑时对应生肖动物为牛，故称“丑牛”。

凌晨3点至5点，属寅时。此时昼伏夜行的老虎最凶猛，古人经常会在这个时段听到虎啸声。因此，寅时对应生肖动物为虎，故称“寅虎”。

清晨5点至7点，属卯时。兔子喜欢吃带有晨露的青草，所以天刚亮它们就出窝了。因此，卯时对应生肖动物为兔，故称“卯兔”。

早晨7点至9点，属辰时。此时一般容易起雾，又值旭日东升，蒸蒸日上之时，而传说中龙最喜腾云驾雾。因此，人们把辰时留给了龙，称此时为“辰龙”。

上午9点至11时，属巳时。此时大雾散去，艳阳高照，蛇类出洞觅食，故称“巳蛇”。

中午11点至1点，属午时。古时野马尚未被人类驯服，喜欢午时四处奔跑嘶鸣，故将此时称为“午马”。

午后1点至3点，属未时。牧羊人认为这是放羊的好时候。因此，古人就把未时与羊对应，故称此时为“未羊”。

下午3点至5点，属申时。此时太阳偏西了，天气凉爽，猴子喜欢在此时爬树啼叫。因此，申时对应生肖动物为猴，故称“申猴”。

下午5点至7点，属酉时。此时太阳落山了，鸡在窝前打转，故称“酉鸡”。

傍晚7点至9点，属戌时。人们劳碌一天，闩门准备休息了。狗卧门前守护，一有动静就汪汪大叫以示警主人，故称此时为“戌狗”。

夜间9点至11点，属亥时。夜深人静，人们能听见猪酣睡的声音，于是将亥时与猪对应，称作“亥猪”。

一天的12个时辰与12个生肖动物就这样匹配

排列下来：子鼠、丑牛、寅虎、卯兔、辰龙、巳蛇、午马、未羊、申猴、酉鸡、戌狗、亥猪。于是中国古人开始使用12生肖对应一昼夜计时，后来又使用12生肖来纪年，从而衍生出丰富多彩的12生肖文化。

三、中国12生肖的文化内涵

中国传统文化的主流是儒家文化，儒家文化的核心内容是“中庸之道”。中庸之道追求不偏不倚、恰到好处，中国成语“过犹不及”便是中庸思想的准确阐释。任何事物都是相对的，即使是优点，过了头便成为了缺点。为此，中国古人依据12个生肖动物的习性特点，将其两两匹配成对，提醒每个人在追求完善自身性格时，需要学习、借鉴其他生肖的性格优点来平衡自身的性格缺陷。在工作和生活中，中国人也希望通过选择与自身性格互补的工作搭档或异性伴侣来实现平衡。这种生肖匹配还具体解释了中国传统文化观念中关于取巧与勤奋、勇敢与理智、高调与低调、进取与谦虚、权变与坚持、随和与忠诚的微妙关系。

1. 鼠和牛配对

老鼠聪明伶俐、机警灵活。老牛的特点则是踏实勤恳、埋头苦干，中国人最喜欢用这样一句谚语来评价牛的奉献精神：“吃的是草，挤出的是奶。”在中国传统文化价值观里，人们既欣赏老鼠的机智取巧，又推崇老牛的踏实苦干精神。如果头脑灵活过了头，容易不喜欢干实事，走向投机取巧；如果只埋头苦干，不懂得做事的技巧和方法，就会事倍功半。因此，聪明的头脑和勤奋能干的品质，二者应完美统一。

2. 虎和兔配对

在中国民间故事里，老虎历来是百兽之王，是勇敢的王者化身；而小兔代表弱小动物，谨慎、理智。如果凡事无所顾忌，勇敢也会变成鲁莽，容易闯祸；而事事过分谨慎，就会缺少克服困难的勇气，就会变得懦弱，无所作为。因此，中国人认为勇敢和谨慎是相辅相成的一对好兄弟。

3. 龙和蛇配对

中国人赋予中华民族创造的神物——“龙”以无上的地位和能力，龙代表的是春风得意和高调；而蛇则是被天庭降罪贬罚到人间的“小龙”，并且丧失了龙的地位和力量，因此蛇成为隐忍、低调的代表。龙和蛇的转换表现出有高潮、有低谷的真实人生，两者的性格特点代表了两个方向，将龙与蛇配对反映出中国人信奉的中庸信条：得志不应骄傲，失意不应颓废。

4. 马和羊配对

自古以来，在中国人的观念中，马是“勇往直前、马到成功”的典型形象。中国人经常把具备这样特点的人比喻为“千里马”，即千里挑一、难得一见的人才；而羊被中国人称道的优秀品质则是谦逊、平和。在汉语中，含有“马”字的成语可能是12生肖动物中最多的，而且绝大多数具有“勇往直前”的意思；羊则是中国民间关于“善良与谦虚”主题故事的主角。因此，中国人希望把马的勇往直前与羊的谦虚平和完美结合起来。

5. 猴和鸡配对

猴子轻巧灵活、善于变化，其智商与人类最接近；而公鸡，无论天气如何，一年365天，每到黎明时分就会打鸣。在古代，中国农民缺少计时工具，往往就以公鸡打鸣作为晨起的信号。因此，中国人把猴子视为灵活权变的典型代表，而公鸡则是持之以恒的代表。中国人一方面赞赏视环境条件不同而随机应变的为人处世观，另一方面又主张持之以恒才能做出成就。因此，猴的灵活权变与鸡的持之以恒应该完美统一。

6. 狗和猪配对

狗对主人十分忠诚，宁可饿死也不会抛弃主人。而猪呢，不择主人，只求吃饱睡好，是顺其自然、随遇而安的典型代表。在中国生肖文化中，狗是忠诚、专一的代表，猪则是财富和幸运的代名词。中国人既推崇狗忠诚而不爱富嫌贫的品质，又羡慕猪不费力气就会拥有财富的幸运。

中国人的价值观是不是有些矛盾呢？可是，这样的矛盾价值观却是中国文化中不可缺少的重要内容。12 种动物的配对，充分体现出中国文化的平衡智慧与追求完美的价值取向。

Chapter Three

A Kaleidoscope of Rat References

Evolution of the Chinese Character 鼠 (Rat)

The evolution of Chinese characters has undergone several phases, namely, the Oracle Bone Script, Bronze Inscriptions, Lesser Seal Script, Clerical Script, Cursive Script, Regular Script and Running Script.

Ancient Chinese characters underwent drastic transformations with changes in writing materials. At the very beginning, characters were inscribed on tortoise shells and animal bones, hence the name 甲骨文 (jiǎgǔwén, the Oracle Bone Script), literally "shell and bone script". Subsequently, in the Zhou Dynasty (1046-256 BC), people inscribed characters on bronze objects which gave birth to and even popularized Bronze Inscriptions to a certain extent. Later on, China split up into seven states (Qi, Chu, Qin, Yan, Zhao, Wei, Han), each with its own characters. When the State of Qin grew in power, it defeated the other six states and unified China. In order to consolidate his rule, the First Emperor of the Qin Dynasty ordered a cancellation of all the characters of the other six states and introduced a unified Chinese character style: the Lesser Seal Script. Like the Oracle Bone Script and Bronze Inscriptions, this writing style still involved complicated characters that were difficult to write. Moreover, people wrote on bamboo slips and wooden boards that were not convenient to carry. According to the historical records, when Dongfang Shuo, a renowned minister during the Western Han Dynasty (206 BC-AD 25), submitted a proposal to the emperor, the bamboo slips were so heavy that they had to be carried by two men into the palace. With the passage of time, Clerical Script came into being, which can be seen as a more concise version of Lesser Seal Script. This marked a major reform in the evolution of Chinese characters. With the introduction of Clerical Script, ancient Chinese characters started their transformation into modern styles. Cursive Script, Regular Script, and Running Script developed from Clerical Script and are considered the major character styles of Chinese calligraphy. In the year 105 during the Eastern Han Dynasty (25-220), a eunuch official named Cai Lun invented the technology that led to the widespread use of paper for writing. Thanks to the introduction of paper, Chinese calligraphy has become an established and popular art form.

Oracle Bone Script

Bronze Inscriptions

Lesser Seal Script

The character 鼠 (shǔ) exists in the style of Oracle Bone Script, which is presented above. It looks like a rat with a pointed mouth, sharp teeth, hunched back, short legs and a long tail. At the top of the character are three dots which represent the rats' preference for food in small pieces. This character is a typical pictograph.

Cursive Script

Clerical Script

Regular Script

Running Script

The form of the character 鼠 evolved as time went by. However, its basic structure in the style of Oracle Bone Script, Bronze Inscriptions and Lesser Seal Script remains the same. After Clerical Script came into use, the character changed a lot and was solidified in the form we see today.

	Oracle Bone Script	Shang Dynasty (1600-1046 BC).
	Bronze Inscriptions	The Spring and Autumn Period and the Warring States Period (770-221 BC).
	Lesser Seal Script	Qin Dynasty (221-206 BC) and Western Han Dynasty.
	Cursive Script	Began in the Western Han Dynasty and became widely used during the Eastern Han Dynasty (25-220), the Sui Dynasty (581-618), and the Tang Dynasty.
	Clerical Script	Widely used at the end of the Western Han Dynasty.
	Regular Script	Began at the end of the Eastern Han Dynasty, became widely used during the period of the Three Kingdoms, the Jin Dynasty (265-420) and the Southern and Northern Dynasties (420-589), and reached its peak during the Tang Dynasty.
	Running Script	Began at the end of the Eastern Han Dynasty, matured during the period of the Three Kingdoms, the Jin Dynasty and the Southern and Northern Dynasties.

Rat-related Idioms, Proverbs, Allegorical Sayings and Songs

Many idioms, proverbs and allegorical sayings in Chinese are related to the rat. Despite Chinese people's aversion to rats, the character 鼠 (rat) is frequently used. According to some statistics, there are more than 40 commonly used Chinese idioms that contain the character 鼠 (rat), relevant folk proverbs and allegorical sayings can also be found in large numbers. Moreover, many art forms have taken the rat as their main character, such as children's songs, folk ballads and even modern pop songs.

I. A selection of rat-related idioms

1. 胆小如鼠

① **Pinyin:** dǎnxiǎo-rúshǔ

② **Literal translation: as timid as a rat**

③ **Meaning: timid, diffident**

There is a story about the origin of this idiom. During the Southern and Northern Dynasties, there was a court official in the Northern Wei State named Yuan Qinghe who was very timid. One day, his subordinate reported to him that troops of the Liang State had reached the city gate and asked for his orders on whether to fight the enemy. Upon hearing that the enemy had come, he trembled with fear and issued an immediate order that all soldiers should lay down their arms. He surrendered to the Liang State and was conferred with the title of the "King of Wei" by the Liang emperor. Several years later, the emperor instructed Yuan to lead an army and launch an attack against Xiangcheng City, the capital of the Wei State. When arriving at the city gate, he was told that the enemy's reinforcements were coming soon. Yuan was so terrified that he issued an immediate retreat. Upon learning of his escape, the Liang emperor flew into a fury and scolded him as a "timid rat". Yuan was then sent into exile in the countryside to raise pigs. This is generally regarded as the origin of the idiom 胆小如鼠 .

2. 投鼠忌器

① **Pinyin:** tóushǔ–jìqì

② **Literal translation: hesitating to pelt a rat for fear of smashing the utensils beside it**

③ **Meaning: holding back from taking actions against an evildoer for fear of harming others**

This idiom also originated from a story from ancient times. There was once a wealthy person who liked collecting antiques very much. One day, a rat got into his favorite jade ware. He was so angry that he picked up a stone and pelted the rat. Unfortunately, he broke his jade, which made him very regretful. He felt guilty for his irrevocable loss due to his impulsive behavior.

II. A selection of rat-related proverbs

Chinese proverbs are short, popular expressions from among the people which demonstrate profound insights. They are often used in spoken language to make it more vivid, expressive and precise.

1. 老鼠过街，人人喊打

① **Pinyin:** lǎoshǔ guò jiē , rén rén hǎn dǎ

② **Meaning: A rat crossing the street is chased by all.**

Given the scarcity of material supplies in ancient China, people then were often in shortage of food and clothing. To them, rats were very harmful animals as they could steal food, chew through clothing and even spread diseases. Therefore, wherever a rat appeared, people would give chase and try to kill it. With the passage of time, the proverb came to indicate that whenever a bad person or an evil deed appears, it will become an object of public condemnation.

2. 老鼠爱打洞，坏人爱钻空

① **Pinyin:** lǎoshǔ ài dǎ dòng , huàirén ài zuān kòng

② **Meaning: While the rat is fond of digging holes, the evil person likes taking advantage of loopholes.**

There is an analogy in this proverb. It is often used in colloquial language to refer to an evil person who likes to seize a chance to seek private gain and even harm others to benefit themselves just like a rat will dig out earth to make a hole.

III. A selection of rat-related allegorical sayings

Allegorical sayings consist of two parts. The first part serves as a clue to a riddle, and the second part as its solution. Under some circumstances, people can figure out the meaning with the clue even without the second part. Therefore, the second part can often be omitted when allegorical sayings are used, hence, the literal meaning of allegorical sayings in Chinese is "the expression that can take a break (in the middle)".

1. 老鼠骑在猫身上——好大的胆子。

① **Pinyin:** lǎoshǔ qí zài māo shēnshang — hǎo dà de dǎnzi

② **Meaning: A rat rides on a cat — being overly audacious**.

Rats and cats are natural enemies, and a rat would shudder at the sight of a cat. In Chinese, this proverb is used to describe someone who is brave and intrepid.

2. 老鼠钻进书堆里——咬文嚼字

① **Pinyin:** lǎoshǔ zuānjìn shūduī li — yǎowén-jiáozì

② **Meaning: A rat gets into piles of books — being nitpicky with words.**

Rats often bite and grind their teeth. This saying literally means a rat gets into a pile of books to bite them. Nowadays, it is often used to describe someone who likes showing off his or her academic knowledge or to satirize someone who overlooks the overall concept of a paragraph or passage of writing by paying undue attention to its diction.

3. 狗逮老鼠——多管闲事

① **Pinyin:** gǒu dǎi lǎoshǔ — duō guǎn－xiánshì

② **Meaning: A dog captures a rat—attend to your own business.**

This allegorical saying originates from an ancient folk story. Long ago, the rapid reproduction of rats led to a disaster in the human world. The rats stole grain and oil for food, and bit people's clothes and possessions; therefore, people abhorred the rats and considered them an evil force, hoping to eliminate them.

Hearing this, the Jade Emperor in heaven decided to dispatch the best rat catcher to exterminate rats for human beings. Unexpectedly, a dog and a cat vied for the task. They argued heatedly, boasting that they were most adept at catching rats. The Jade Emperor was caught in a dilemma and decided to ask the cat and the dog to annihilate the rats together. Whoever killed more rats would be conferred the title "Rat Hunter General", and rat-catching would become the lifelong career of his family and their offspring.

After arriving in the human world, the dog and the cat lived in a dilapidated temple. Since the rats often engaged in nocturnal activities, the dog and the cat rested in the temple in the daytime and hunted for the rats at night. They promised if a rat was caught, they would bite its tail off and put it in cloth bags so that they could count the numbers by the number of tails.

At the outset, the dog caught almost as many rats as the cat. But later on, the situation changed. The dog, on its way to catching rats, often helped people to look after their possessions. When noticing a thief stealing something from a person who was sound asleep, the dog would dash at the thief and tear at his clothes. Meanwhile, the dog would bark at the owner to awaken him. However, the cat devoted all its energy to rat-catching, so there were more and more rat tails in its cloth bag.

With the concerted efforts of the dog and the cat, the rat disaster was defused. Then they returned to the palace in heaven to meet the Jade Emperor with their cloth bags. Seeing the tails in their bags, the Jade Emperor granted the cat the title of "Rat Hunter General" and the cat family followed in its footsteps to continue catching the rats. The dog was conferred the title of "Guardian of the Courtyard", so guarding residences became the career of the dog family.

From then on, the dog and the cat had their own jobs. The dog was responsible for guarding residences while the cat would search everywhere at night for the rats who were ready to eat the grain in the barn.

However, the dog would still catch rats occasionally, doing what the cat should do. So when people say 狗逮老鼠 (A dog catches a rat), it means "attend to your own business".

IV. A selection of rat-related folk ballad and song

The rat also plays an indispensable role in Chinese literature and music. Almost every child can sing a folk ballad or nursery rhyme that is about the animal. "Little Rat Climbing the Lampstand" is a household ballad that has been passed down through generations. Here are the interesting lyrics:

Little rat is climbing onto the lampstand.

He gets there for some tasty oil but is unable to come down!

He begins squeaking for his grandma.

But she is nowhere to be found.

Having no way out, he has to roll down from the stand!

A love song titled "Rat Loves Rice" caused quite a stir in China.

When such animals are written into popular songs, it proves that the Chinese zodiac constitutes an important part of people's lives. The following is an excerpt from "Rat Loves Rice".

I love you, my dear,
Just like the rat loves rice.
I will accompany you in spite of the wind and rain.
I miss you, my dear,
No matter how hard life is,
I will do everything to make you happy.
I love you so much...

Rat-related Chinese Folk Tale — "Rats Marrying off Their Daughter"

A Chinese folktale claims that according to the Xia calendar, the third day of the first month is when rats get married. Therefore, each and every household should go to bed very early in order not to disturb this joyous occasion. If the rats are disrupted on this day, they will seek revenge against mankind. Just like the saying goes: "If disturbed by men on my big day, I (rat) will make them suffer for a whole year." The following is one version of the story:

光明

Long, long ago, there was a happy family of three: Mother Rat, Father Rat and their daughter. Their daughter was the apple of their eye; so much so, that they set their mind on finding her a husband who would be the most capable and powerful one in the world.

Having lived in a cold, damp and dark hole for many years, the couple wanted to create a much better living environment for their daughter so that she could enjoy sunshine and blue skies.

One night, Dad and Mom were lying in bed, discussing with each other who the most powerful being in the world was. However, a whole night of debate produced no real results. The day broke with the first ray of sunshine shining over their hole. Dad became overjoyed and shouted, "There is no one more suitable than Mr. Sun! He is the most powerful because he shines upon the earth and can bring warmth to the whole world."

Hence the couple set off for the east to where the sun rises in the hopes of finding their perfect son-in-law. They basked in the warm sunshine throughout the journey, which strengthened their will to marry their beloved daughter to Mr. Sun.

The couple finally found Mr. Sun on a mountaintop in the east. They proposed to him and said, “Great Sun, marry our daughter, and you will be blessed with a happy life.”

Upon hearing their proposal, Mr. Sun replied with a smile and said, “Actually, I’m not as powerful as you imagine. A dark cloud can shut out all my light. You’d be better off with him as your son-in-law!”

Disappointed, the rat parents found some measure of truth in what he said, “Mr. Cloud not only produces rain and snow to nurture the land, but he can also block the sunshine. He is indeed the most powerful." Therefore, they headed for a valley to the north where Mr. Cloud resided.

They arrived at the northern valley and proposed marriage to Mr. Cloud. He replied with an awkward smile, "Even though I have the power to shut out the sunshine, I could be dispelled even by a gentle wind. Plus, I am unable to block Mr.Sun without Mr. Wind's help. You'd better ask him to be your son-in-law!"

The couple were disappointed again, but for the sake of their daughter, they set out again to look for Mr. Wind.

It was an arduous journey for the rat couple in search of Mr. Wind. As someone who often wandered around, Mr. Wind had no fixed address. The couple had to ask around and chase Mr. Wind. After a hard search, they finally found him at the end of a desert in the west.

They brought up the marriage proposal again. However, Mr. Wind burst into laughter and said, "Even though I can blow away the dark cloud, I can do nothing in front of a wall other than move around him! Moreover, I'm such a wanderer, so I

回避
囍

have no home at all. You'd better ask Mr. Wall to be your son-in-law!"

Under Mr. Wind's guidance, Rat Dad and Mom headed south and found a high and thick wall. Mr. Wall was terrified to see them and said, "To me, you rats are the most fearful creature in the world! No matter how solid I am, I will collapse sooner or later because of rat holes."

In astonishment, Rat Dad and Mom realized that rats are indeed the most powerful! After their encounter with Mr. Wall, the couple discussed with each other and Dad came up with an idea, "Then who are we fearful of? Oh, I know! Cats have been our natural enemies ever since ancient times! Our daughter should marry a cat!" Hearing this, Mom became worried, "We can't do that! How can you marry our daughter to our enemy?" Dad explained to her, "Don't worry! After becoming our son-in-law, the cat won't be our enemy any longer and will stop eating us."

Thus the rat parents went to the Yellow Weasel to invite him to be the matchmaker and propose marriage to Cat. To everyone's surprise, Cat readily agreed to the proposal. The next day, Cat invited Weasel to his home for dinner. They had a joyful chat, but Cat soon got drunk. He told Weasel, "I will eat Rat's daughter soon after I marry her! How can I turn down such a treat!"

Upon returning from Cat's, Weasel immediately disclosed Cat's real intention to the rat couple. They were scared into a cold sweat. Only then did the rat parents say, "There are no perfect husbands in the world! Even the most capable must have their shortcomings. As rats, we also possess our unique strength. Our vanity and greed almost cost our daughter's life!"

Having realized their fault, the couple then chose a handsome young rat to be their son-in-law. He was very smart and capable. On the evening of the 3rd day of the first month of the Xia calendar, the rat parents held a grand wedding ceremony for their beloved and beautiful daughter.

This popular folktale, “Rats Marrying off Their Daughter”, has been passed down in China for thousands of years. The story has long become an enduring theme for artists in their work. Many art forms such as New Year pictures, clay sculptures, and paper-cuts are based on it.

十二生肖

第三章 生肖鼠趣谈

一、“鼠”的字形演变

简单总结中国文字的演变，大致经历了甲骨文—金文—小篆—隶书—草书—楷书—行书等几个主要阶段。

中国古文字的变迁是伴随着书写载体的变化而变化。最早人们把文字刻在龟甲兽骨上，所以称为“甲骨文”。到了周朝时期，人们在金属钟鼎器具上铸文，金文出现并得到一定推广。周朝后期，中国开始动荡，逐渐分裂成七个诸侯国，他们各有各的文字。后来秦国逐渐强大起来，并最终战胜六国，统一了中国。为了便于统治，第一个皇帝——秦始皇取消其他六国的文字，创制了统一的汉字书写形式，即小篆。小篆与甲骨文、金文字形一样，仍然很复杂，书写不易；加之当时的人们一般是在竹简、木板上书写，十分不方便。史书记载，中国西汉时期的名臣东方朔给皇帝提的建议写成竹简需要两个成年男子抬进皇宫去。这种情况下，小篆渐渐向简便快捷的方向演变，逐渐形成了隶书。隶书在中国汉字发展史上是一个重大的变革，从隶书开始，古代汉字的字形基本接近于现代汉字。后来中国书法作品主要的字体形式草书、楷书、行书均从隶书演化而成。105 年，中国东汉宦官蔡伦发明造纸术，纸张自此逐渐被广泛应用。因为纸张的使用，中国书法才得以成为一门普及而成熟的艺术门类。

汉字“鼠”在甲骨文中就有，字形就是一只非常形象的老鼠：尖嘴、利齿、弓背、短腿和长尾，最上方还有三个点，代表着老鼠喜欢吃的碎小食物，属于典型的象形字。

“鼠”字在漫长的岁月演变中字形字体不断变化。甲骨文、金文和小篆字体没有改变其象形字的根本，从隶书开始字形发生较大变化，奠定了此后多种字体的基础。

	甲骨文	商朝
	金文	先秦时期
	小篆	秦、西汉
	草书	始于西汉，兴盛于东汉、隋唐
	隶书	兴于西汉末期

鼠	楷书	始于汉末，兴于三国两晋南北朝，盛于唐朝
鼠	行书	始于汉末，成熟于三国两晋南北朝

二、与鼠相关的成语、谚语、歇后语及歌曲

在汉语中，有很多以老鼠为主角形成的成语、谚语和歇后语。虽然老鼠不是中国人喜欢的动物，但是“鼠”字出现的频率还是挺高的。据不完全统计，在汉语中，含有“鼠”字的常见成语就多达40多个，相关的民间谚语和歇后语也为数不少。此外，还有很多以鼠为主角的儿歌、民谣，甚至还有当代流行歌曲。

1. 与鼠相关的成语

（1）胆小如鼠

胆子小得像老鼠那样。形容人胆小怕事，很不自信。

关于这个成语还有一个历史故事呢。中国南北朝（420—589）时，有一个北魏朝廷的官员名叫元

庆和，他十分胆小。有一天，他的手下来报告，敌方梁朝的军队已经到达城外，是否要与敌方开战。他一听敌人来了，吓得浑身发抖，急忙下令所有的将士放下兵器，投降了梁朝。于是梁朝皇帝册封他为“魏王”。几年后，梁朝皇帝命令元庆和带兵去攻打项城。当他带兵到达项城城外时，还没等开战，只听说马上有援军到来，他就吓得马上下令撤退。梁朝皇帝得知这个消息，大骂元庆和胆小如鼠，然后把他贬到乡下养猪去了。“胆小如鼠”成语也就由此而来了。

（2）投鼠忌器

本意为要打老鼠又怕打坏了它旁边的器物而犹豫不决。比喻想打击坏人却有所顾忌。

这个成语也出自一个历史故事。古代时有一个喜欢收藏古董的富人。他看到一只老鼠钻到他最喜欢的玉器里去了，非常生气，毫不犹豫地拿起一块石头去打老鼠，没想到把心爱的玉器打碎了。他非常难过，并为自己一时的冲动行为带来不可挽回的损失而深深自责。

2. 关于鼠的谚语

中国谚语是形成于民间的固定语句，用简单通俗的话反映出深刻的道理。谚语多使用在口语中，以增加语言的生动性、形象性和准确性。

（1）老鼠过街，人人喊打

古时候的人们物质匮乏，缺衣少食，而老鼠总偷吃食物，还常咬碎衣物，传播疾病，对人有害无益。因此，只要看到老鼠出现，人们就会纷纷追打。这句谚语后来引申为一旦出现坏人坏事，就会引起大家一致的痛恨。

（2）老鼠爱打洞，坏人爱钻空

这是一句采用类比手法的中国谚语。人们在口语中常常用老鼠喜欢掏土打洞的习性来讽刺那些总喜欢投机且做出损人利己之事的坏人。

3. 关于鼠的歇后语

中国歇后语由前后两部分组成：前一部分起“引子”的作用，像谜面；后一部分像谜底。在一定的语言环境中，通常当说话者说出前半截，听话者就可以领会和猜想出它的本意，常常可以“歇去”后半截，所以就把这样的句子称为“歇后语”。

（1）老鼠骑在猫身上——好大的胆子

因为老鼠与猫是天敌，老鼠一见到猫就会吓得浑身颤抖，所以中国人用老鼠骑在猫身上来形容人的胆子变得非常大，无所畏惧。

（2）老鼠钻进书堆里——咬文嚼字

老鼠有咬东西磨牙的习性，表面意思是老鼠钻进书堆里啃咬书本。现在人们使用这个歇后语来形容一些人说话时故意卖弄学识，有时候也用来讽刺那些写文章过分斟酌字句而忽略整段或整篇文章思想的人。

（3）狗逮老鼠——多管闲事

这个歇后语来自一个古老的民间传说故事。相传很久以前，老鼠家族因繁殖太快，老鼠多得成灾。它们偷吃人们储藏的粮食和油，咬坏人们的衣物、用品，因此，人们非常憎恨老鼠，把它们当成了人间的祸害，总想消灭它们。

天上的玉皇大帝得知这件事后，决定选派捕鼠能手去人间帮助人们灭鼠。没想到，狗和猫都来争抢这项使命。它们吵得面红耳赤，都说自己是捉老鼠的能手。玉皇大帝有点左右为难，最后决定：让狗和猫一起去人间灭鼠。灭鼠多者，就封为“震鼠将军”，其家族从此以后世代以捉老鼠为业。

狗和猫来到了人间后，住进一座废弃的破庙里。因为老鼠总喜欢夜里出来活动，所以狗和猫就白天在庙里休息，晚上外出捉老鼠。它们约定：抓住一只老鼠，就咬断它的尾巴，放进布口袋，最后以老鼠尾巴来计数。

刚开始，狗和猫每天捕捉的老鼠数差不多。可是，后来事情就有了变化，狗去捉老鼠的时候，还顺便帮助人们看护财产。当它发现有小偷趁着人们熟睡去偷东西时，狗就冲上去撕咬小偷的衣服，还“汪汪”大叫，唤醒被偷人家的主人。而猫一心一意地捉老鼠，布口袋里的老鼠尾巴越来越多。

在狗和猫的努力下，人间的鼠害终于平息了。它们带着各自的布口袋回到天宫见玉皇大帝。玉皇大帝下令封猫为“震鼠将军”，今后猫的家族世代以灭鼠为业；封狗为“护院将军”，今后狗的家族世代帮助人们看家护院。

从此，狗和猫便有了明确的分工：狗帮助人们看家护院；猫呢，夜里四处巡逻，专逮那些准备偷吃粮仓里粮食的老鼠们。

可是狗空闲的时候也常常捉捉老鼠。因为捉老鼠本来应该是猫的工作，所以就有了“狗逮老鼠——多管闲事”的说法。

4. 关于老鼠的民谣、歌曲

在中国民间口头文学和音乐艺术中，老鼠也是不可或缺的重要角色。每一个中国孩子都能随口背上一首关于老鼠的民谣。《小老鼠上灯台》就是在中国传承久远、家喻户晓的一首儿童民谣。歌词诙谐有趣：

小老鼠，上灯台，
偷油吃，下不来，
吱儿吱儿叫奶奶，
奶奶也不来，

叽里咕噜滚下来。

中国流行歌坛曾经有一首爱情歌曲《老鼠爱大米》唱遍中国大地。这反映了在中国生肖观念深入人心，老鼠也可以入歌。部分歌词如下：

我爱你，爱着你，
就像老鼠爱大米，
不管有多少风雨我都会依然陪着你。
我想你，想着你，
不管有多么的苦，
只要能让你开心我什么都愿意，
这样爱你……

三、关于鼠的中国民间故事
——老鼠嫁女

中国民间传说中，夏历正月初三是老鼠娶亲的日子。这一天的晚上家家户户要早早上床睡觉，以免打扰了老鼠的亲事。原因在于老鼠在娶亲这天如果被打扰，就会报复人类。中国有句谚语："人闹我（鼠）一天，我（鼠）闹人一年"。故事梗概如下：

很久以前，有一个幸福的三口之家：鼠妈妈、鼠爸爸和鼠女儿。鼠妈妈和鼠爸爸把女儿视为心肝宝贝。它们决心要为女儿寻找一个天下最有本领、最了不起的新郎。

老鼠一家常年住在阴湿寒冷的黑洞里，夫妻俩想为女儿创造一种更好的生活环境，摆脱这种看不见阳光和蓝天的生活。

一天晚上，鼠爸爸和鼠妈妈躺在床上商量谁才是天下最有本领的。他们争论了整整一夜也没有结果。天亮了，清晨第一束阳光照在老鼠洞口。鼠爸爸高兴地差点跳起来，大声说："就是太阳！太阳是最了不起的！他普照万物，能温暖全世界。"

于是，鼠爸爸和鼠妈妈急急忙忙向着东方出发了，去太阳升起的地方寻找太阳去了。一路上，阳光灿烂，温暖地照在它们身上，这更加坚定了他们要把女儿嫁给太阳的想法。

他们终于在东方的山顶找到了太阳。他们向太阳提亲："伟大的太阳，请你娶我们的女儿吧！你们一定会很幸福的。"

太阳听了鼠爸爸和鼠妈妈的请求，微笑着回答说："我没有你们想象的那样伟大，一片乌云就可以遮住我的光芒。你们还是去找乌云做女婿吧！"

鼠爸爸和鼠妈妈听了太阳的话，虽然有些失望，可是又觉得有道理："乌云可以变成雨雪，滋润大地，连太阳都能遮挡，还是乌云最有本领。"于是，他们又向着乌云居住的北方山谷出发了。

鼠爸爸和鼠妈妈来到北方的山谷，向乌云提亲。乌云苦笑着回答："尽管我有遮挡太阳光芒的力量，

但是只要有一阵轻风，就可以让我‘云消雾散’。就连遮挡阳光这件事也需要风先生配合我才能办到啊。你们还是去找风先生做你们的女婿吧！”

鼠爸爸和鼠妈妈又一次失望了，可是为了女儿的幸福，他们又不辞辛苦地出发去寻找风先生了。

为了寻找风，鼠爸爸和鼠妈妈找得好辛苦。因为风先生是位流浪汉，他居无定所。鼠爸爸和鼠妈妈只好到处打听，到处追逐，好不容易才在西方的沙漠边上找到了风先生。

鼠爸爸和鼠妈妈又一次提亲，没想到风先生哈哈大笑起来：“我是可以吹散乌云，但是只要有一堵墙就让我无能为力，只能在墙前打转转！我四处流浪，也没有自己的家，你们还是去找墙先生做你们的女婿吧！”

于是，鼠爸爸和鼠妈妈在风先生的指引下，向南方出发，找到了一堵又高又厚的墙。墙看到他们，有些害怕地说道：“在这个世界上，我最怕你们老鼠，任凭再坚固的墙也抵挡不住老鼠打洞，最终都会坍塌。”

鼠爸爸和鼠妈妈听到这话非常吃惊：看来还是咱们老鼠最有力量。在墙那碰壁后，鼠爸爸跟鼠妈妈商量："我们老鼠又怕谁呢？啊，对了！老鼠自古以来就怕猫！咱们的女儿应该嫁给猫。"鼠妈妈担心地说："不行，不行！我们和猫世世代代都是天敌，怎么能把女儿嫁给猫呢？！"鼠爸爸解释说："没关系的，猫做了我们的女婿，以后就不会再与我们为敌，吃我们老鼠了。"

就这样，鼠爸爸和鼠妈妈找到了黄鼠狼，请他做媒人去向猫提亲。没想到猫一听说这事，毫不犹豫地答应了下来。第二天，猫请黄鼠狼到他家里做客喝酒，因为太高兴，猫喝醉了，得意地对黄鼠狼说："等我娶了老鼠的女儿，就吃掉她，美美地饱餐一顿，谁让他们自己送上门的！"

黄鼠狼回来后，赶紧把猫的真实想法告诉了鼠爸爸和鼠妈妈。鼠爸爸和鼠妈妈听了黄鼠狼的话，吓得出了一身冷汗，这才恍然大悟："原来世界上没有十全十美的人，本领再强的人也有弱点，我们老鼠也有长处。我们差点儿因为自己的虚荣和贪念断送了女儿的性命。"

醒悟了的鼠爸爸和鼠妈妈后来为女儿选择了一

只年轻英俊、聪明能干的老鼠做女婿。就在中国夏历的正月初三这天晚上，鼠爸爸和鼠妈妈用最隆重的仪式送最美丽、最心爱的女儿出嫁。

这就是在中国民间流传千百年、人人耳熟能详的老鼠嫁女的故事。这个故事成为民间艺人进行艺术创作经久不衰的重要题材。在中国民间艺术年画、泥塑、剪纸等不同形式中产生了大量的艺术作品。

Chapter Four

The Rat in Chinese Indigenous Art

Rat-themed Chinese Paintings

I. Chinese Traditional Paintings

The traditional Chinese painting style involves using a water-dipped brush to draw on silk or paper with ink and watercolor. Human figures, landscapes, birds and flowers are common subjects for traditional Chinese painting.

Ever since ancient times, the Chinese zodiac has been an important subject in paintings. When the Year of the Rat comes around, rats become the centerpiece of works by Chinese painters and folk artists.

Zhu Zhanji (1398-1435), the fifth emperor of the Ming Dynasty, was adept at painting rats. His paintings "Bitter Gourd and Rat" and "Lychee and Rat" are considered masterpieces.

In the painting "Bitter Gourd and Rat", there is a big rock with strong, resilient grass and elegant bamboo at the bottom of the image. Exuberant vines of a bitter gourd wind themselves over the bamboo branches. A rat stands ready on the rock to reach for the big and heavy bitter gourd that hangs overhead in the gentle breeze. The lingering aroma from the gourd makes the rat eager to taste it. As the main character in the painting, the rat is rendered a delicate profile in light ink with strong strokes for its whiskers and very dark ink for its bright piercing eyes. In front of this exquisite and lifelike painting, one can easily feel the rat's desire for the bitter gourd and will be deeply impressed with its lively gaze.

The painter portrayed a typically abhorrent rat as an adorable one: sensitive, reasonable and a little mischievous, very different from the type of rat people usually want to hit when it crosses a street. Zhu Zhanji was the first emperor to regard the rat as a positive image for artistic creation. At the time, Zhu had few male offspring to carry forward his lineage, a perplexity for an emperor. Many people believe the reason why he beautified the rat is that it symbolizes strong fertility. He created an adorable image of the rat with his superb painting skills. Apart from the rat, there is a bitter gourd with a lot of seeds in this painting. Both the rat and the bitter gourd, one being an animal and the other a plant, are prolific, therefore symbolizing the prolificness of the emperor's lineage. Zhu painted the work "Bitter Gourd and Rat" to celebrate the arrival of his newborn son, hoping for a greater progeny. It is regrettable that he stayed in power for only 10 years and died before the age of 40.

In the painting "Lychee and Rat", a rat stands firmly in the middle of the frame with his eyes staring ahead and tail slightly curled. In front of the rat are three lychees and leaves with a

good blend of red and green.

In contemporary times, traditional Chinese painting master Qi Baishi, who was born in the Year of the Rat, created a lot of works related to rats. Among the rats he painted, some are lively and clever, while others are cunning, greedy and funny. These vivid images are so popular with the public that Qi is jokingly called the "Rat Painting Expert". It is said that when Qi's favorite painting, "Rat Bites the Book", a work he created in the 1930s, was stolen by someone who also liked the painting, he painted another one. The second painting included an inscription describing the whole story related to the loss of the previous work.

Nowadays, some painters try to combine the methods of traditional Chinese painting and cartoons, like the cartoonist Hua Junwu. His work, "Rat Talks Big", satirizes those who like telling lies or saying empty words. This work has had great influence since it was published and was later donated to the National Library of China.

II. Chinese New Year Paintings

Chinese New Year Paintings are traditional folk paintings

in China that have enjoyed a long history. Most works are characterized by their concise drawing style, bright colors and explicit meanings. This has made them very popular among the Chinese people.

Chinese New Year Paintings thrived during the Qing Dynasty, which gave rise to many hubs such as Yangliuqing Town in Tianjin; Yangjiabu Village in Weifang, Shandong Province; Wuqiang County, Hebei Province; Zhuxian Town in Kaifeng, Henan Province; Fengxiang County, Shaanxi Province; Taohuawu in Suzhou, Jiangsu Province; Mianzhu City, Sichuan Province and Tantou Town in Shaoyang, Hunan Province. Given the different geographical conditions, historical and cultural backgrounds, social customs as well as aesthetic views, Chinese New Year Paintings from various regions often feature different local characteristics.

Chinese New Year Paintings are usually printed and put up during the Spring Festival, which is the most important festival each year. The zodiac is always a popular theme.

New Year Woodblock Prints, a traditional printing handicraft, are a specific type of Chinese New Year Painting. They date back to the Northern Song Dynasty (960-1127) when

movable-type printing was invented. Movable-type printing is considered one of the four great inventions in ancient China (i.e., gunpowder, paper, the compass and printing). The woodblock printing procedures go as follows: The painter draws a picture on a thin piece of paper and places it on a woodboard with the image reversed. Then an engraver will use a variety of metal knives to carve wood boards according to the picture. The picture's color will determine what type of wood board is needed. If the picture has only one color, one wood board is enough. But if the picture has more than one color, two types of wood boards are needed, namely the ink plate and the color plate. The ink plate is used to print the outline of the picture while the color plate is used to color the picture. The number of color plates is determined by how many colors the picture has. After the ink plates are made, the engraver applies the ink to the ink plate, puts a piece of white paper of a certain size on the plate and presses the paper with a palm fiber brush. The outline of the picture will then be printed on the paper. Next, the color plates are carved one by one according to the area of a certain color in the picture, and its colors are printed on the paper in the way mentioned above. In this way, the wood carving paintings can be mass produced.

A typical woodblock print related to the rat is one called "Rats

Marrying off Their Daughter", whose story was introduced in the previous chapter. The woodblock print has different versions in different regions across China.

Rat-themed Sculptures and Porcelain

I. Sculptures and sugar figurines

Nowadays, various sculptures based on the Chinese zodiac culture are common scenes in China. You can often find a lot of zodiac sculptures in parks, scenic spots, playgrounds, city streets and shopping districts. Hongluo Temple, a famous Buddhist temple in Beijing, even has a designated zodiac spot for tourists.

The renowned Chinese artist Huang Yongyu has been dubbed "a Wizard" for his artistic talent. He has taken a fancy to creating artistic works related to the rat. Huang was born in 1924, the Year of the Rat. When the Year of the Rat came in 2008, Huang created the sculpture "The Joy of Rat". The sculpture sees a rat grinning with a pipe in its mouth. It stands with its two feet wide apart with its left hand on its hip and eyes narrowed. It seems as if the rat is intoxicated by mellow pipe smoke. The rat is the incarnation of the creator, Huang Yongyu, who has an ardent love of smoking.

Among the zodiac statues, "Twelve Zodiac Animal Heads from Yuanmingyuan (Old Summer Palace)" is the most renowned in the world. It used to serve as the sprinkler of a time-signaling fountain. These heads would spray water for a designated period of time in turn. Each animal represents a "double hour" and would spray water for those two hours. At noon, the 12 sprinkler heads would spray water simultaneously, forming a spectacular scene. Unfortunately, after the Yuanmingyuan was set on fire in 1860, these bronze statues drifted overseas. Happily, in recent years, some of them have been recovered and returned to China. The rat and rabbit statues were the first cultural relics repatriated to China and are now preserved in the National Museum of China.

In addition, in China's folk society, there is another handicraft called sugar figurines, which dates back to the end of the Ming Dynasty and the beginning of the Qing Dynasty. A sugar figurine is made of boiled liquid sugar. The liquid sugar is applied to the end of a straw, through which the creator exhales to make the liquid sugar balloon while kneading and twisting it to form a variety of shapes. Then a bamboo pick is used to put the figurine aside for cooling. Sugar figurines come in the shape of animals, especially the twelve zodiac animals. An artist will often make a sugar figurine into the shape of the zodiac animal that corresponds to the year in which the customer was born or the year that they are currently in. For example, a creator will often make a sugar figurine shaped like a rat for a child born in the Year of the Rat.

Nowadays, children have more and more toys and food, so sugar figurines are not as popular as they used to be. However, they are still considered a form of folk art greatly valued by the public. At Beijing temple fairs, many visitors from other countries have also shown great interest in this art form.

II. Porcelain wares, cloisonné and wine culture

Chinese porcelain has a long history that can be traced back to the Shang Dynasty during the 16th century BC. Along with silk, Chinese porcelain has been a focal point of Chinese culture. After the Tang Dynasty, porcelain wares made during the Song,

Yuan (1206-1368), Ming and Qing dynasties had established themselves all over the world for their exquisite workmanship and relevant techniques; porcelain manufacturing techniques have been passed down to modern times. Nowadays, famous porcelain cities and towns, such as Jingdezhen, Jiangxi Province; Dehua, Fujian Province; Yixing, Jiangsu Province; Foshan, Guangdong Province; Zibo, Shandong Province and Tangshan, Hebei Province are still developing these traditional techniques.

The rat is small and adorable and ranks first among the 12 zodiac animals, so rat-themed porcelain is quite popular with Chinese people. This type of porcelain has been produced for thousands of years. Chinese zodiac porcelain pieces are mostly artifacts and ornaments; while some are for daily use, such as the animal ornaments on china tea sets and children's coin banks.

Like porcelain, cloisonné is one of the famous artistic handicrafts in China. It also goes by the name enamel. It is made by folding copper wires into different decorative patterns before soldering them on metalwork. This divides the object's surface into compartments. These compartments are then filled with enamel. The cloisonné is finished after final heating. Historical records show that the original technique was introduced into China from Arab nations at the end of the 13th century. After gradual evolution during the Yuan, Ming and Qing dynasties, a unique cloisonné culture was formed.

Zhang Tonglu, a contemporary cloisonné master in China, created the serial work "12 Zodiac Animals Cloisonné". This work was exhibited in the China Pavilion at the Shanghai World Expo in 2010 and won great acclaim both at home and abroad. The following is one piece from the work: "12 Zodiac Animals Cloisonné: Rat". Each cloisonné in this series is composed of three parts: top, body and base. The top resembles the Temple of Heaven, where ancient Chinese used to offer sacrifices to gods, and indicates the will of heaven. The body is covered with the images of the 12 zodiac animals and indicates the harmony of human beings. Since the dragon and rain symbolize auspiciousness and good harvest according to China's traditions, the dragon and rain images on the base symbolize abundance in the years to come. This work of art is representative of the harmonious unity of heaven, earth and human beings embodied in China's traditional culture. This work also shows the superb workmanship required in producing cloisonné.

The combination of China's liquor culture with the zodiac animals has a long history. In ancient China, there were bronze and porcelain liquor vessels in the shape of zodiac animals. Nowadays, many liquor factories produce zodiac animal themed liquor each year for commemoration or collection before the Spring Festival. Supply often runs out quickly. This kind of liquor features the zodiac animal image and calligraphy on the package and a bottle shaped like a zodiac animal. The top liquor brands in China, Maotai and Wuliangye (Five Grain Liquid) produce rat-themed liquor in the Year of the Rat. The liquor bottle looks like a rat, which indicates the year when the liquor was produced. Zodiac animal liquor has become a characteristically Chinese collector's item.

Rat-themed Paper-cuts

Paper-cuts are made by using scissors or knives to cut images or patterns in pieces of paper. Paper-cutting is a Chinese folk art form that often adds flair to not only local community activities but also everyday life. In China, paper-cutting has a long history and is very popular among the people. It has become an essential part of various folk activities. In May 2006, this traditional art was included in the National Intangible Cultural Heritage List. At a meeting held by the United Nations

Educational, Scientific and Cultural Organization (UNESCO) in September and October 2009, Chinese paper-cutting was selected into the Representative List of the Intangible Cultural Heritage of Humanity.

The paper-cutting tradition started at the beginning of the Tang

Dynasty, became popular in the Song Dynasty and reached its peak during the Ming and Qing dynasties. Paper-cuts fall into the following eight categories based on the patterns that appear on them: the human figures, birds and other animals, Chinese characters, household utensils and containers, flowers and plants, fruits and vegetables, insects, and the natural landscape. They feature images of praying for blessings, dispelling evil forces, admonishing others and fun living.

Chinese paper-cutting art mainly consists of two schools, the South School and the North School. Foshan, Guangdong Province; Wuhan, Hubei Province; Yangzhou, Jiangsu Province and Zhangpu, Fujian Province are the birthplaces of the South School of Chinese paper-cutting, while the North School is best known for the pieces produced in Yuxian County, Hebei Province; Gaomi, Shandong Province and other localities in Shanxi and Shaanxi provinces. It's worth mentioning that Gaomi, Shandong Province is the hometown of Mr. Mo Yan, the renowned Nobel laureate in Literature.

The Chinese consider the Spring Festival to be their most important festival, thus it is accompanied with grand celebrations. Paper-cut window decorations featuring the 12 zodiac animals have been an important way for the people to mark the occasion for generations. The rat ranks first among the 12 zodiac animals, and thus it is quite important. Because of its longevity and strong fertility, people have created a lot of paper-cut works related to the rat with the hope of more offspring and blessings, such as "The Rat Eats Grapes" and "The Rat Eats the Ears of Wheat". When the Year of the Rat approaches, most people will put up a pair of paper cuts with the theme of the rat on the interior of the windows in their houses, praying for more offspring and prosperity of their families.

The Rat in Works of Chinese Literature

The image of the rat has been seen in works of Chinese literature since ancient times. *Classic of Poetry* is the oldest existing collection of Chinese poetry and contains a lot of works related to the rat. One poem that saw some of the most wide-spread appeal, called "Large Rats", is presented below. In Chinese literature and traditional operas, the rat always represents the exploiting class or a robber.

Large Rats (Excerpt)

Large rats! Large rats!
Do not eat our millet.

Three years have we had to do with you.

And you have not been willing to show any regard for us.

We will leave you.

And go to that happy land.

Happy land! Happy land!

There shall we find our place.

— *translated by James Legge*

The connotation of the rat didn't change until the Ming Dynasty. *The Story of the Three Heroes and Five Gallants* is regarded as a pioneering work of China's swordsman fiction.

In this classic Ming novel, there are five chivalrous men called the "Five Rats", which are nicknamed Earth-piercing Rat, Mountain-boring Rat, River-overturning Rat, Sky-penetrating Rat, and Brocade-coated Rat respectively. Despite their great mastery of martial arts, they are forced to steal and be involved in fraudulent activities because of their impoverished life. The episode "Five Rats Make Trouble in the Capital" is the climax of the novel. It recounts how the "Five Rats" travel to the capital of Dongjing for a martial arts competition, where Justice Bao persuades them into redressing misconduct and practicing justice, so as to serve their country. This story spread far and wide and has been adapted for Peking Opera, local opera, film, and TV.

Rat-themed Postage Stamps

Zodiac animal stamps constitute an important part of China's zodiac culture. With an ever increasing influence of China's culture in the world, many countries issue stamps related to the zodiac animals during the Spring Festival. Japan issued its first set of zodiac animal stamps in 1950.

In China, the first zodiac animal stamp, "Monkey Stamp", was issued in 1980. The whole set of the 12 zodiac animal stamps became available for the first time with the release of the "Goat Stamp" in 1991.

The first "Rat Stamp" was issued in 1984. The adorable rat on the stamp was created by China's renowned cartoonist Zhan Tong. This rat has eight visible whiskers, a pair of big ears and a thin tail curled up. With its eyes open wide, it appears greedy, but smart and humorous. In the cartoon picture, this rat is no longer the one abhorred by people, but the one who stands apart with its small claws in front, seeming to send New Year greetings.

This stamp is of great value for collectors because the rat ranks first among the 12 zodiac animals and this is the first rat-themed stamp issued in China. In 1984, 80 of the rat-themed stamps (one package) had the nominal value of 6.40 yuan, while one package today commands a market price of 4000 yuan, demonstrating the strong appreciating value of the stamps over time.

China issued three versions of the rat-themed stamp in 1984,

1996 and 2008 respectively. The version in 1996, with the theme of "city lights", shows a standing rat with a lamp stand in its hand. The stamp has become an item that Chinese philatelists strongly seek since it came out. In the same year, the United States Postal Service issued a rat-themed stamp with a nominal value of 32 cents to celebrate China's lunar New Year of the Rat. The middle of the stamp features the image of a golden rat; while on the upper right and left side are the English words "HAPPY NEW YEAR" and the characters " 鼠年 " in the cursive style.

Before and after the Spring Festival in China, local post offices issue zodiac animal postmarks with zodiac animal images and words. They are often stamped on letters or commemorative posted items.

第四章 关于鼠的中国本土艺术表现形式

一、关于鼠的中国绘画

1. 中国国画

中国国画采用毛笔蘸水、墨、彩作画于绢或纸上。人物、山水、花鸟等是中国国画的主要题材。

12 生肖题材的绘画在中国自古至今都是一个重要的绘画题材。每逢鼠年到来时，生肖鼠就会成为中国画家和民间艺人们绘画作品中的的主角。

中国明代第五位皇帝朱瞻基（1398—1435）是中国绘画史上的一位画鼠高手，他的《瓜鼠图》《荔鼠图》等作品被认为是上乘佳作。

《瓜鼠图》左下角绘有一巨石，旁边生长着坚韧耐磨的牛筋草和清韵雅致的劲竹；繁茂的苦瓜藤蔓，缠着竹枝，盘绕而上；一只老鼠站在石头上跃跃欲试，想吃头顶上随风微摆的苦瓜。肥厚硕大的苦瓜刺激着嗅觉灵敏的老鼠，令它垂涎三尺。老鼠通体淡墨，胡须勾勒精细，笔力强劲；浓墨下的眼睛，炯炯有神，生动异常。整个画面栩栩如生，灵动活泼，它恨不能一口咬下苦瓜——瞧它那副顾盼自如的神态，真的令人过目难忘。

画者朱瞻基将人人憎恶的老鼠描绘得可爱至极，令读者看到的不是人人喊打的过街老鼠，而是通灵性、却又不乏小淘气的精灵。朱瞻基应该是第一个将老鼠作为美好形象来进行艺术创作的皇帝了。很多人认为，朱瞻基之所以美化老鼠，是因为他遇到了皇家最大的困惑，即子嗣不旺、当须努力的局面。而老鼠恰恰有超强的生育能力，一胎多子，代表着繁衍昌盛。于是，朱瞻甚运用生花妙笔，化丑恶为美丽，赋予老鼠可爱的形象。图画中，与多子老鼠相映成趣、相得益彰的是瓤籽繁多的苦瓜。一个是动物，一个是植物，它们都有超强的生命力，这预示着皇室香火不绝，长盛不衰。朱瞻基绘《瓜鼠图》正是为了纪念他喜得龙子的幸福时光，同时也寄望以后子嗣繁盛，枝繁叶茂。令人感到惋惜的是，他在位只有 10 年，不到 40 岁就死了。

他的另一幅画《荔鼠图》笔墨处理比较简洁，画面上老鼠居中，鼠眼正视，尾巴平上略曲，鼠的前方有三颗荔枝，三片叶子，红绿相间。

到了近代，国画大师齐白石先生也有许多鼠画作品传世，可能与他属鼠有关。他笔下的老鼠有的活泼机灵，有的狡猾取巧，有的贪婪可笑，个个生动鲜活，令人捧腹不已，广受喜爱，也因此得了个“鼠画家”的戏称。据说，在20世纪30年代，齐白石先生创作过一幅《鼠子啃书图》，老人自视为得意之作。没想到，没多久就被别人因为喜欢而顺走了。齐白石于是又重作一幅，并在第二幅作品上题字数行，述说这件事情的缘由。

到了当代，一些画家开始尝试将中国传统绘画与漫画相融合的创作方法，比如著名漫画家华君武创作的《老鼠吹牛图》，讽刺了当时人们爱说假话、大话、空话的社会风气。该作品一经发表，就在当时产生了较大影响。后来他将此画捐献给了中国国家图书馆。

2. 中国年画

中国年画是拥有悠久历史的一种传统绘画形式，其特点是绘制简单、色彩鲜艳、寓意直白，深受百姓喜爱，在民间流传非常广泛。

中国年画在清代高度繁荣，逐渐形成一些年画集散地，如天津的杨柳青镇、山东潍坊的杨家埠村、河北的武强县、河南开封的朱仙镇、陕西的凤翔县、江苏苏州的桃花坞、四川的绵竹，以及湖南邵阳的滩头镇，等等。不同地区的年画因地理环境、历史文化、世俗风尚、审美趣味的不同而呈现出鲜明的地方特色。

中国年画往往在中国人一年中最重要的节日——春节时印制并张贴。每一年的主题少不了生肖年画，因此，12 生肖成为中国年画重要且不可缺少的创作主题。

木版年画是中国年画中一种古老的手工印刷传统工艺，其根源可以追溯到中国古代的四大发明之一——北宋时期发明的活字印刷术。具体制作方法是：画师先在薄纸上绘制图画，然后将薄纸反贴在木板上，由刻工使用各种金属刀具在木板上雕刻成形。刻工需要根据画师绘制的图画是单色还是多色来决定雕刻几块木版：如果是单色画就只需雕刻一块木版；如果是多种颜色就需要雕刻两种木版。第一种只有一块，用于印制图画的线条轮廓，一般使用黑色油墨，所以称作“墨版”。另一种称作“色版”，根据图画颜色多少决定刻制多少块色版。墨版和色版刻好后，印工们就可以在刻工雕刻好的墨版上涂上油墨，然后将已裁剪好固定尺寸的白纸放置在墨版上，用棕毛刷按压白纸，木板上雕刻的图案线条轮廓就印在了白纸上。然后继续按照这样的做法，使用不同色版给年画的空白部分添加红、黄、蓝等颜色。如此就可以批量印制同一图案的年画了。

在关于老鼠主题的中国木板年画中，最常见的作品就是我们前面介绍过的“老鼠嫁女”，也被称作“老鼠娶亲”。在中国知名的木版年画生产地，都有不同形式的木版年画。

二、关于鼠的雕塑和陶瓷

1. 鼠的雕塑和吹糖人

关于12生肖主题的民俗文化雕塑作品在中国十分普遍，各类公园、旅游景点、儿童乐园，以及一些城市的街道、商圈、步行街等地方常常会发现关于12生肖主题的雕塑作品，甚至在北京红螺寺内这样的佛教圣地也设有专门的12生肖雕塑景观区。

中国知名美术家黄永玉先生被国人称为“鬼才”。他十分偏爱创作生肖鼠的美术作品。2008年是中国的鼠年，出生于1924年的黄永玉属鼠，他创作了一尊“快乐之鼠”的雕塑作品。铜鼠口衔烟斗，咧嘴大笑，左手叉腰，八字脚开立，眼睛微眯，仿佛陶醉在一口口香醇良烟中——俨然就是嗜烟如命的黄永玉。

关于12生肖的雕塑作品，在全世界最为有名的当属“圆明园12生肖兽首铜像”。他们曾是圆明园中报时喷水池中的报时喷头，每个动物代表一个时辰，每到一个时辰，相应的动物喷头就会喷水两个小时。正午时分，12个喷头一起喷水，景象颇为壮观。可惜后来随着圆明园被烧，这些铜像流落到了海外。值得高兴的是，这几年已有多件铜像回到了中国，其中鼠首和兔首是首批回归中国的文物，现存放在中国国家博物馆。

中国还有一项特殊的民间工艺——吹糖人。吹糖人技艺大约始于明末清初，制作时把糖稀熬好，用一根麦秸杆挑上一点糖稀，再对着麦秸杆吹气，糖稀随即像气球一样鼓起，然后通过捏、转等手法配合吹起塑成各种造型。最后用竹签挑下，冷却后成型。糖人以动物造型居多，最常见的便是12生肖。艺人一般根据顾客的属相或当年生肖年来制作生肖糖人。例如，一个属鼠的孩子来买糖人，一般会吹塑一个老鼠形状的糖人。

如今，儿童的玩物和食物多了，糖人不再是孩子们爱不释手的玩物和吃食，而是作为一项民间艺术受到重视。现在在北京年节的庙会上还可见到吹糖人表演，许多外国友人对此比较感兴趣。

2. 鼠的陶瓷作品及其他艺术形式

中国陶瓷制作历史悠久，可以追溯到公元前16世纪的商代。中国陶瓷曾经一度与丝绸一起成为中国文化的代名词。尤其是唐朝以后的宋、元、明、清代的瓷器以精美绝伦著称于世，陶瓷制作延续至今。江西景德镇、福建德化、江苏宜兴、广东佛山、山东淄博、河北唐山等都是当代中国知名的陶瓷之城。

鼠因为是12生肖中排在第一位的生肖，而且老鼠体型小巧可爱，所以鼠形陶瓷艺术作品深受广大中国人民的喜爱，千百年来老鼠陶瓷作品不断出现。中国12生肖陶瓷作品大多为艺术摆件和玩物，但也有部分作品具有实用性，如茶具上的陶瓷宠物、儿童陶瓷储钱罐等。

除了陶瓷制品，景泰蓝也是中国著名的特种工艺品之一。景泰蓝正名“铜胎掐丝珐琅”，俗名“珐蓝”，又称“嵌珐琅”，是一种在铜质的胎型上，用柔软的扁铜丝掐成各种花纹焊上，然后把珐琅质的色釉填充在花纹内烧制而成的器物。据史料记载，13世纪末，该技术由阿拉伯国家传入中国，后历经元、明、清三个朝代的不断改进，形成了独特的景泰蓝文化。

中国景泰蓝界大师张同禄先生创作的“景泰蓝12生肖尊”作品在2010年的上海世博会中国主题馆展出时，曾引起不小的轰动。就拿生肖尊——子鼠为例：它以天坛为顶暗含“天意”，以12生肖环绕鼎身，象征“人和”，祥龙布雨于地风调雨顺，寓意“地丰”。此套作品完美阐释了中国传统文化天、地、人三者完美合一的核心观念，也彰显出中国人制作景泰蓝的最高技艺。

中国生肖与酒文化相结合诞生的生肖酒文化也有很长的历史。在古代就有生肖动物形状的铜质酒器和陶瓷酒器。今天，许多酒厂每年春节前都会推出生肖主题的纪念酒或收藏酒，而且出现一瓶难求的情况。其主要表现是在外包装上以图画、书法等艺术形式表现生肖主题，酒瓶采用特种工艺制成生肖动物的形象。例如最知名的中国白酒品牌——茅台和五粮液两家公司就在鼠年推出了鼠年酒，一个老鼠外形的酒瓶暗含了酒的生产年份。生肖酒也成了收藏市场的一种中国特色的藏品。

三、关于鼠的剪纸

中国剪纸是用剪刀或刻刀在纸上剪刻花纹或图形，用于装点生活或配合其他民俗活动的一种民间艺术。在中国，剪纸具有悠久历史和广泛的群众基础，是各种民俗活动的重要组成部分。2006 年 5 月，剪纸艺术被列入中国第一批国家级非物质文化遗产名录。2009 年 9–10 月，在联合国教科文组织保护非物质文化遗产政府间委员会第四次会议上，中国剪纸项目入选“人类非物质文化遗产代表作名录”。

中国剪纸的流行始于唐朝初期，宋代在民间普及，明清两代空前兴盛。中国剪纸根据纹样图案可以大致分为人物、鸟兽、文字、器皿、花木、果蔬、昆虫、山水等八类，主要表现纳吉祝福、驱邪除恶、劝勉警戒、生活趣味等主题。

中国剪纸流派主要分南、北两派，南派剪纸发祥地主要有广东佛山、湖北武汉、江苏扬州、福建漳浦等地。北派剪纸以河北蔚县、山东高密、山西和陕西等地剪纸最为出名。山东高密是中国第一位获得诺贝尔文学奖的莫言先生的家乡。

春节是中国人最重视、最隆重的节日，因此，用于春节的12生肖窗花剪纸是中国人世代相传、永恒不变的主题。鼠作为12生肖的第一个生肖，位置重要，加之老鼠寿命长、繁殖力强，民间创作了很多祈求多子多福的作品，比如老鼠吃葡萄、老鼠吃麦穗，等等。鼠年来临时，多数人家喜欢在屋内的玻璃窗上贴一副鼠主题的窗花剪纸，祈愿鼠年子孙满堂、家族兴旺。

四、中国文学作品中的鼠形象

中国文学作品中自古就有老鼠的形象。中国最早的诗歌集《诗经》就有多篇关于老鼠的作品，其中流传最广泛的是一篇名为《硕鼠》的诗歌。从此，老鼠在中国文学作品和戏曲舞台上常以剥削阶级或盗窃者的形象出现。

《硕鼠》（摘选）

硕鼠硕鼠，无食我黍！三岁贯女，莫我肯顾。
逝将去女，适彼乐土。乐土乐土，爰得我所！

老鼠的形象到了明代开始有所改变。明代古典名著《三侠五义》被认为是中国武侠小说的开山之作。书中有五位身怀绝技的侠士，他们分别被称为

“彻地鼠”“穿山鼠”“翻江鼠”“钻天鼠”和“锦毛鼠”。他们个个身怀绝技，但因生活所迫，常常做些偷鸡摸狗、坑蒙拐骗之事。《五鼠闹东京》是书中的高潮段落，讲述了这五鼠兄弟闯到当时的都城东京参加比武，后被官员包拯感化而改掉恶习，开始行侠仗义、为国尽力的故事。此故事在中国民间流传广泛，可谓妇孺皆知。在中国多种艺术形式中几乎都有这个故事的表现形式，如京剧、各种地方戏、古装影视剧，等等。

五、关于生肖鼠的邮票

生肖邮票也是中国生肖文化体现的一个重要领域。随着中国文化影响力的扩大，世界上很多国家在中国春节期间开始发行生肖邮票。日本于 1950 年发行首套生肖邮票。

中国第一枚生肖邮票——“猴票”发行于 1980 年，到 1991 年发行“羊票”后，第一轮生肖邮票共计 12 枚全部出齐。

第一套鼠年邮票在 1984 年发行，图案选自中国著名漫画家詹同创作的一只有趣、可爱的老鼠。这只老鼠嘴上八根胡须清晰可数，有一双大大的招风耳，细长的尾巴趾高气昂地向上翘着，小眼睛炯炯有神又那么贪婪地瞪得溜圆，显得机灵、诙谐。经过漫画手法的处理，这只老鼠不再是人人喊打的可憎之物，而是两腿站立。一双弯弯的小爪在胸前微微拱起、神情幽默、仿佛在向人们祝贺新年的小宠物。

这枚邮票极具收藏价值，因为鼠是12生肖动物的首位，且是中国发行的第一张鼠年邮票。1984年一整版鼠年邮票（80枚）面值为6.40元人民币，现在市场价格涨至4000元人民币，其收藏价值可见一斑。

截至2018年，中国邮政一共发行了三轮生肖鼠年邮票：1984年鼠票、1996年鼠票、2008年鼠票。其中1996年鼠票上是一只站立的老鼠端灯台的形象，主题为“万家灯火”。这枚邮票一问世就成了中国邮票收藏者追捧的明星邮票。同年，美国联邦邮政总局为庆祝中国农历鼠年特别发行鼠年邮票：邮票面值32美分，中间是金黄色的老鼠图案，右上角有英文“HAPPY NEW YEAR”，票面左侧是用草体书写的两个汉字——“鼠年”，非常醒目。

在中国，各地邮局在春节前后还会推出个性化的生肖邮戳，形式多由生肖动物形象加文字构成，在信件或纪念邮品上加盖。

Appendix:

Table of Chinese Zodiac Animals and Their Corresponding Christian Years (1912—2031)

shǔ
鼠

1912	1972
1924	1984
1936	1996
1948	2008
1960	2020

niú
牛

1913	1973
1925	1985
1937	1997
1949	2009
1961	2021

hǔ
虎

1914	1974
1926	1986
1938	1998
1950	2010
1962	2022

tù
兔

1915	1975
1927	1987
1939	1999
1951	2011
1963	2023

lóng
龙

1916	1976
1928	1988
1940	2000
1952	2012
1964	2024

shé
蛇

1917	1977
1929	1989
1941	2001
1953	2013
1965	2025

mǎ
马

1918 1978
1930 1990
1942 2002
1954 2014
1966 2026

yáng
羊

1919 1979
1931 1991
1943 2003
1955 2015
1967 2027

hóu
猴

1920 1980
1932 1992
1944 2004
1956 2016
1968 2028

jī
鸡

1921 1981
1933 1993
1945 2005
1957 2017
1969 2029

gǒu
狗

1922 1982
1934 1994
1946 2006
1958 2018
1970 2030

zhū
猪

1923 1983
1935 1995
1947 2007
1959 2019
1971 2031

责任编辑：翟淑蓉
英文编辑：吴爱俊
英文审定：龚燕灵 James Hutchison
封面设计：厚　冬
责任印制：汪　洋

图书在版编目（CIP）数据

生肖鼠 ： 英、汉 / 张立章编著. -- 北京 ： 华语教学出版社, 2018.10
（中国生肖文化解读系列）
ISBN 978-7-5138-1629-8

Ⅰ. ①生… Ⅱ. ①张… Ⅲ. ①汉语－对外汉语教学－语言读物 ②十二生肖－文化
Ⅳ. ①H195.5②K892.21

中国版本图书馆CIP数据核字(2018)第194817号

本书获得北方工业大学出版基金的资助，在此表示感谢。

中国生肖文化解读系列 · 生肖鼠

张立章 编著

华语教学出版社有限责任公司出版
（中国北京百万庄大街24号　邮政编码 100037）
电话: (86)10-68320585 68997826
传真: (86)10-68997826 68326333
网址: www.sinolingua.com.cn
电子信箱: hyjx@sinolingua.com.cn
北京玺诚印务有限公司印刷
2019 年（32开）第1 版
2019 年第1 版第1 次印刷
（英汉）
ISBN 978-7-5138-1629-8
定价: 49.00元